Critical Listening Skills
For Audio Professionals

by

F. Alton Everest

⁞⁞ COURSE TECHNOLOGY
CENGAGE Learning™

Australia • Brazil • Japan • Korea • Mexico • Singapore • Spain • United Kingdom • United States

Critical Listening Skills for Audio Professionals

Publisher and General Manager, Course Technology PTR: Stacy L. Hiquet
Associate Director of Marketing: Sarah O'Donnell
Manager of Editorial Services: Heather Talbot
Marketing Manager: Mark Hughes
Executive Editor: Mike Lawson
PTR Editorial Services Coordinator: Elizabeth Furbish
Cover Designer & Interior Layout Tech: Stephen Ramirez
CD-ROM Producer: Mike Lawson
Indexer: Katherine Stimson

Audio recording Fred Bogert: Studio C Productions
System 5 mixing console cover image courtesy Euphonix.

ISBN-10: 1-59863-023-7
ISBN-13: 978-1-59863-023-7
Library of Congress Catalog Card Number: 2006923225

7 11 10

COURSE TECHNOLOGY
CENGAGE Learning™

Course Technology PTR, a division of Cengage Learning
25 Thomson Place
Boston, MA 02210
www.courseptr.com

Acknowledgments

The very wide scope of this book has involved the cooperation of many individuals to whom I offer my sincere gratitude. Special thanks to Dr. Edward Carterette, Professor of Psychology, University of California, Los Angeles, for checking the accuracy of the psychoacoustical concepts. Special thanks also to Carol Plantamura, Professor of Music, University of California, San Diego. The Auditory Perception section bears the imprint of the genius of Ron Streicher, Pacific Audio-Visual Enterprises, Monrovia, California. Ron is known for his international leadership in the Audio Engineering Society and as co-director of the Audio Recording Institute of the Aspen Music Festival. My deepest gratitude is also expressed to the staff of Cardinal Business Media Inc. for their patience as well as their competence in bringing this project to completion.

F. Alton Everest

About the Author

The late **F. Alton Everest** (1909-2005) was the most respected audiologist in the professional recording industry. His revered works and courses produced more than twenty books and editions in his lifetime, including *The Master Handbook of Acoustics*, *Audio Techniques for the Home and Studio*, and *How to Build a Small Budget Recording Studio from Scratch ... With 12 Tested Designs*. As the supervisor of UC San Diego's Listening Section Laboratory during WWII, Everest conducted underwater sound research experiments for the war effort. For 25 years he produced science films for the renowned Moody Institute of Science, followed by years teaching and working as a highly sought after audio consultant.

Contents

CONTENTS

BOOK 2 Auditory Perception

Preface

The world of recorded music is dominated by equipment such as amplifiers, loudspeakers, and other electronic paraphernalia. We recognize that our precious music signal can be degraded when passing through such devices. After all our fancy measuring equipment has been employed, we must depend on our ears for the final answer to the question, "Is the sound quality acceptable?"

The maestro on the podium, the recording engineer, and the experienced music critic have sufficiently trained ears for such a judgment. But how about the student just learning about the mysteries of sound recording? The ears of the maestro, the engineer, the music critic, and the student would probably be equally sensitive if tested by the friendly local audiologist. The difference is that the student does not have the critical listening experience of the others.

This book is based on the premise that through subjection to scores of listening experiences similar to those that trained the sound engineer's ears, the student can rapidly and effectively accelerate his or her critical listening ability. The first half of this volume (Book 1: "Critical Listening") is devoted to exercises in estimating changes in sound frequency, sound level, band limitations and irregularities, distortion, noise, etc.

The second half of the volume (Book 2: "Auditory Perception") is devoted to a study of the human auditory system—psychoacoustics, if you will. The same approach used in Book 1 is used in Book 2 to present masking effects, the auditory filters (critical bands), delayed sounds and perception of non-linearities in the ear, what makes some sounds consonant and some dissonant, and other important effects.

This teaching/learning method is effective, as was proven by the enthusiastic reception accorded the *Critical Listening* package (manual and audio cassettes) released in 1982 and the *Auditory Perception* package (manual and audio cassettes) issued in 1986. These are now out of print, but this re-issue includes all of their information in a single volume. With compact disc sound, it promises to be a solid contribution for the future.

BOOK 1

Critical Listening

Ten Lessons Designed for
Instruction in Critical Listening

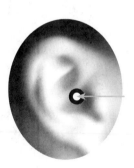

Introduction to Critical Listening

"Golden" Ears

Listening intently, the sound engineer deftly makes a small adjustment to one of the many console channels before him. He registers satisfaction at what has been accomplished by that tiny change. A bystander might listen hard without detecting any change whatsoever in the sound. Observing the sound engineer at work over a period of time would give a person a keen appreciation of his skill and artistry.

How did he get this ability? It was built up by listening experiences which came one at a time, incident after incident, day after day, year after year. Many different types of sound problems were encountered: distortion, imbalances in frequency responses, traces of noise, etc. Over the years, the sound engineer's sensitive ears and keen memory stored an organized file of what constitutes good, clean music and what can creep in to degrade it.

Training in Critical Listening

The following audio training course in critical listening can be the basis for an individual to develop a truly discriminating listening ability. This is accomplished through listening to a carefully devised series of "sound bytes" that emulate what the sound engineer experiences over a period of many years. In other words, the amazing ability of the sound engineer to discriminate can be broken down into a number of simple parts that can be taught and learned.

This course is designed to accelerate, not replace, the usual slow learning process on the job. A series of specific listening experiences in auditory discrimination, arranged in a logical and organized form, is the heart of this training course. As a byproduct, the student will get a "crash course" in audio technology and electronic terminology.

Technical Support

Listening is a psychophysical, subjective activity. Listening critically inevitably relates the activity to physical things such as amplifiers, microphones, loudspeakers, and environment. In this volume, the listening experiments are accompanied by pertinent technical information, providing a technological anchor to the highly subjective process of listening to music. Flaws heard in the music are not a curious, evanescent phenomenon; a solid scientific reason for the flaw is sought. In this way, the subjective listening experience is constantly related to the physical technology involved. This amounts to brief and painless instruction in audio engineering vocabulary and technology along with instruction in critical listening.

The printed text of this book is identical to the narration on the CD (compact disc) sound recording. This affords great flexibility in using the package for individual or classroom use. A useful classroom program would introduce a lesson to the assembled class and provide a subsequent assignment for individual students to go through one or more times in a study carrel.

Estimating the Frequency of Sound

Pure tones and random noise

Talk   **Tech**

To deal effectively with various audio systems, we must have a thorough understanding of the frequency spectrum of signals to be handled by these systems. Speech and music, our usual signals, are so very complex it is often necessary for us to break them down into tones or narrow bands to understand them better.

> **DEFINITION**
> **Spectrum:** the distribution of the sound energy throughout the audible frequency range

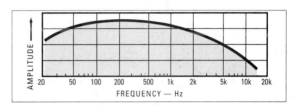

> **EXAMPLE:**
> Spectrum of the sound of typical rock music

The frequency range of audible sound is commonly taken as 20 Hz to 20,000 Hz.

> **DEFINITION**
> **Frequency:** The number of cycles per second = the number of hertz.
> k = kilo = 1000
>
> 1 kHz = 1000 Hz
> 10 kHz = 10,000 Hz
> 20 kHz = 20,000 Hz

Talk **Tech**

To avoid problems commonly associated with the extremes of the audible band, we will keep within a 100-Hz limit at the low end and 10,000-Hz limit on the high end.

If you cannot hear these extreme tones, it may be either the fault of your ears or the fault of your equipment.

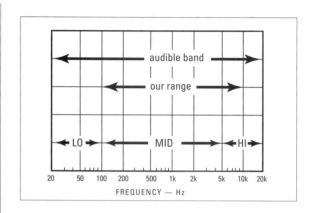

This is a 100-Hz tone:

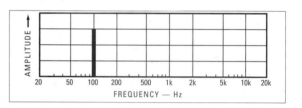

This is a 10,000-Hz tone:

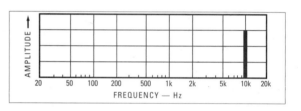

They differ only in the rapidity of oscillation of the air particles which bring the sound to your ears.

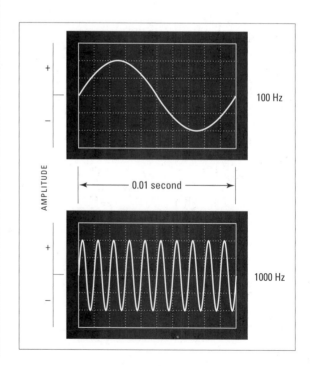

Talk   **Tech**

Now, let us listen to a few other tones as we travel up through the audible range of frequencies between 100 Hz and 10,000 Hz.

Here is the 100- Hz tone again:

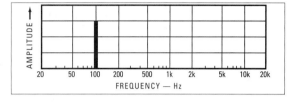

This is a 260-Hz tone, which corresponds closely to the middle C on the piano. But of course, it does not have the richness of the piano tone:

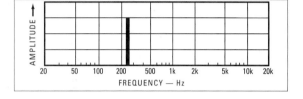

Increasing the frequency, we move up the scale one octave to the C above middle C, twice 260 or 520 Hz:

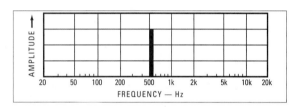

DEFINITION

Octave: If one tone has twice or half the number of vibrations per second as another tone, the two tones are one octave apart.

Talk

Tech

This is 1000 Hz:

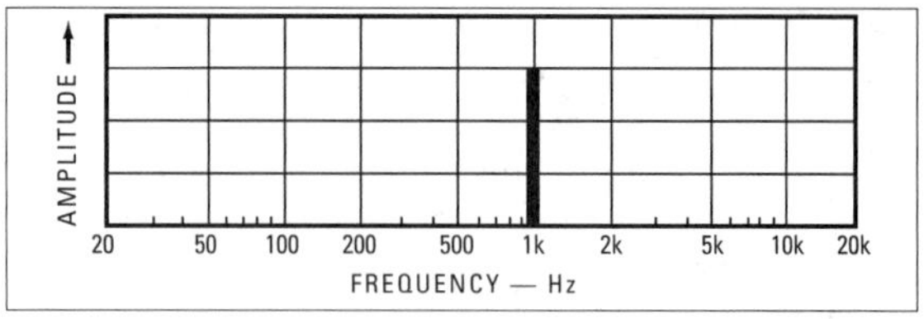

This is 5000 Hz:

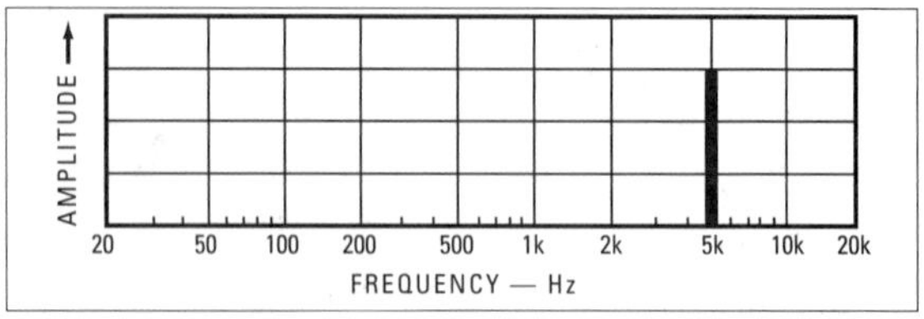

Now for a sweep of tones through the entire audible spectrum. Don't be concerned about the fluctuations in loudness you hear:

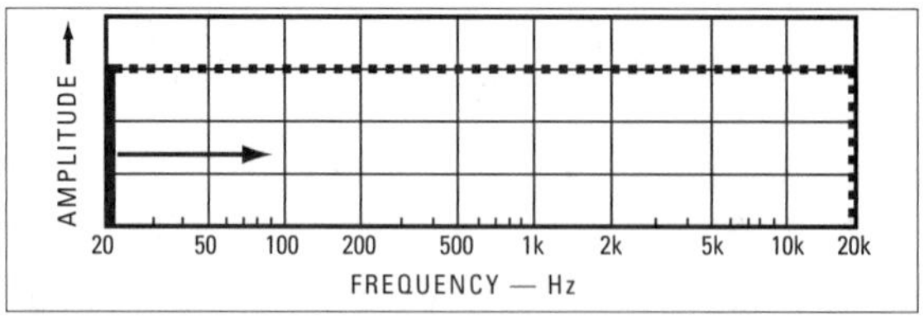

Pure tones (that is, single frequencies) carry little information alone, but they represent the essential building blocks of all speech and music with potential for carrying a tremendous amount of information.

DEFINITION
Pure Tone = single frequency

In some ways, random noise is actually closer to speech and music signals than pure tones. Random noise is constantly shifting in frequency, amplitude, and time relationships.

In the manual, you can see a cathode ray oscillogram of a pure sine wave, the simplest of all signals, and random noise, which is far more irregular and constantly shifting.

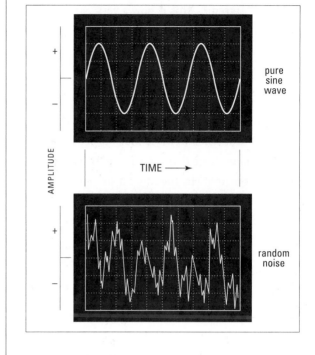

Let's listen to a sample of random noise which has energy distributed through the entire audible band from 20 Hz to 20,000 Hz:

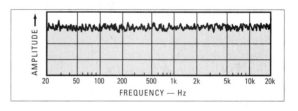

A band of noise one octave wide, centered on 1000 Hz, extends from about 700 Hz to about 1400 Hz. Here is a sample of an octave band of noise centered on 1000 Hz:

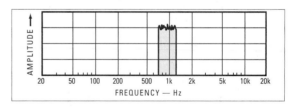

Now, let's consider a band of noise one-third octave wide centered on 1000 Hz. This band extends from about 890 Hz to about 1100. Here is a sample of a noise band one-third octave wide:

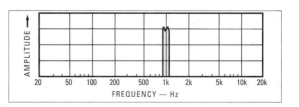

Going to extremes, this is how a very narrow band of noise only one-tenth octave wide sounds:

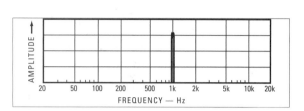

We shall now listen to these four noise bands in succession. Note that the narrower the band centered on 1000 Hz, the more it sounds like 1000 Hz:

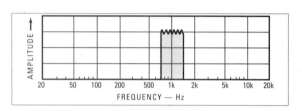

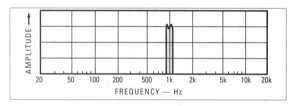

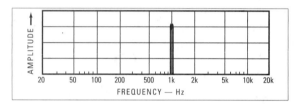

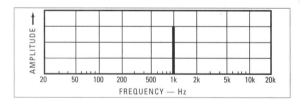

For review, here is wide-band random noise spanning the entire audible range of frequencies:

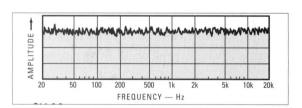

Now we are going to hear this band divided into pieces one octave wide:

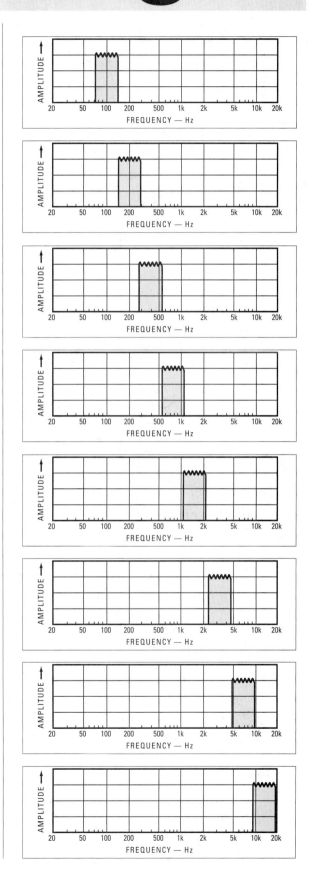

Talk   Tech

The eight octaves of noise we have just heard were centered on the following frequencies:

100 Hz:

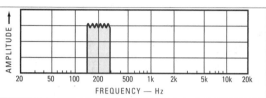

200 Hz:

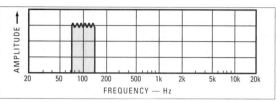

400 Hz:

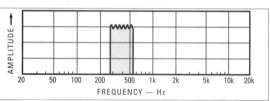

800 Hz:

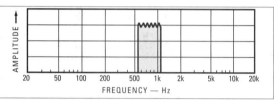

1600 Hz:

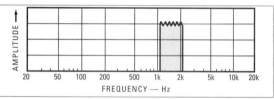

3200 Hz:

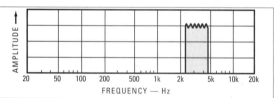

6400 Hz:

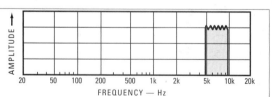

and 12,800 Hz:

Note that the frequency doubles each time, hence the spacings are by octaves.

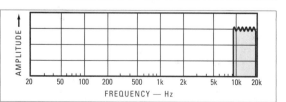

Noise bands are useful in acoustical measurements in rooms because their constantly shifting nature, strange as it seems, gives steadier readings than pure tones. Pure tones, on the other hand, are commonly used in equipment measurements.

People with perfect pitch ability are able to identify musical notes with great accuracy. There are very few people with such ability, but everyone can learn to make at least rough estimates of the frequency of tones. For practice, let's listen to tones of different frequencies to sharpen our ability to distinguish between them.

First, 1000 Hz:

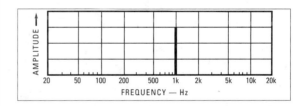

This is 500 Hz:

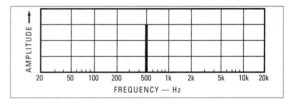

Again, 1000 Hz:

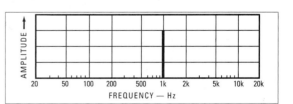

Talk | **Tech**

2000 Hz:

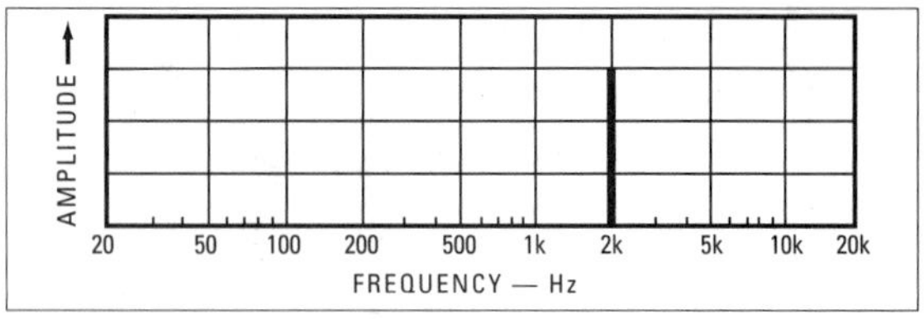

5000 Hz:

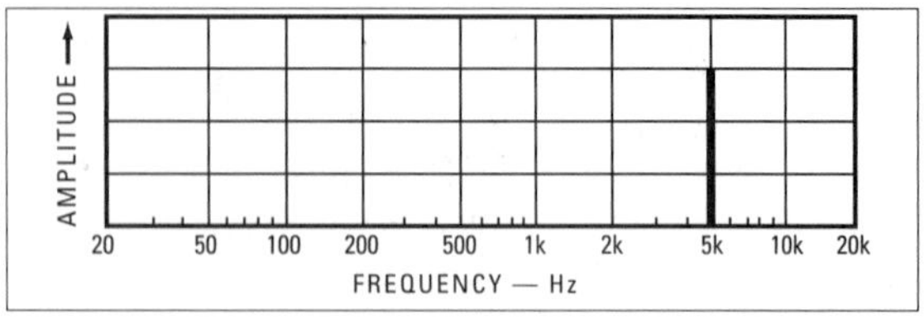

10,000 Hz:

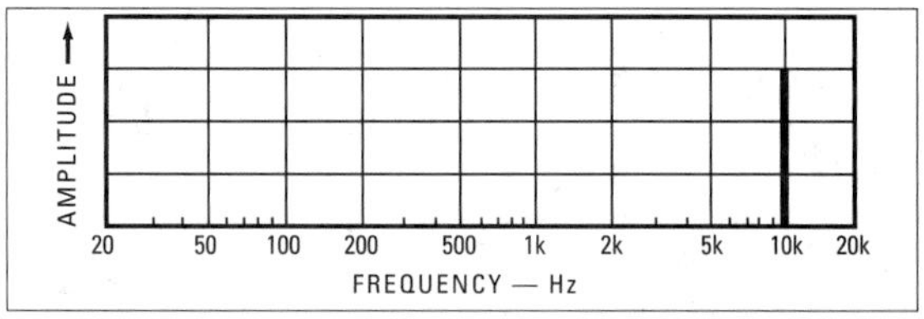

Using only these six tones, can you identify each one as they are presented in a mixed order? Try it!

Sound A:

Sound B:

Sound C:

Sound D:

Sound E:

Sound F:

Jot down your estimates:

____

____

____

____

____

____

Talk | Tech

Let's see how close you came.

Sound A: 1000 Hz

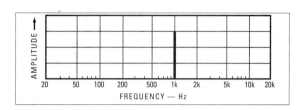

Sound B: 500 Hz

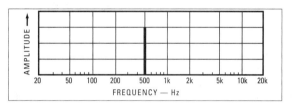

Sound C: 5000 Hz

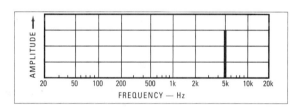

Sound D: 100 Hz

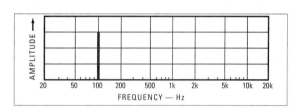

Sound E: 2000 Hz

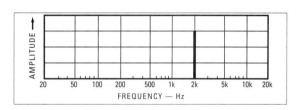

Sound F: 10,000 Hz

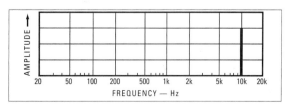

Talk

Tech

Now for a bit of practice in estimating tones in between the previous six tones. See how close you can get in this test.

Sound G:

Sound H:

Sound I:

Sound J:

Sound K:

Sound L:

Jot down your estimates:

_____

_____

_____

_____

_____

_____

Talk   Tech

This test required estimating the frequency of tones in between those we have heard earlier in this lesson. Let's see how well you were able to do this.

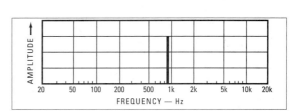

The first sound, Sound G, was 800 Hz:

Sound H was 250 Hz:

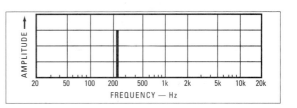

Sound I was 1500 Hz:

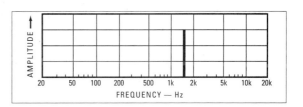

Sound J was 6000 Hz:

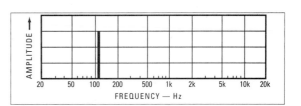

Sound K was 120 Hz:

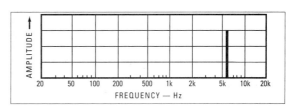

And the last tone, Sound L, was 3000 Hz:

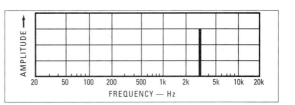

This concludes Lesson 1. Go back over this lesson to sharpen your ability of estimating frequency.

Estimation of Sound Level Changes

Tones, speech, and music

Talk   **Tech**

It is often necessary to estimate how much a sound level changes. Our ear interprets sound level changes as changes in loudness. The decibel is a very convenient unit for measuring signal levels in electronic circuits or even sound pressure levels in air. However, changes in the loudness of sounds as perceived by our ears do not conform exactly to corresponding changes in sound level.

DEFINITIONS

Sound Level: a physical quantity (measured with instruments)

Loudness: a psycho-physical sensation perceived by the human ear/brain mechanism

Decibel: one-tenth of a bel, which is the logarithm of the ratio of any two power-like quantities

Logarithm: (common log to base 10) of a number is the exponent of 10 that yields that number

EXAMPLES

$$\text{Sound pressure level, dB} = 20 \log \frac{\text{(sound pressure in question)}}{0.00002 \text{ pascal (the reference pressure)}}$$

Sound	Measured sound pressure	Sound pressure level
Rustling leaves	0.0002 pa	20 dB
Riveter	20 pa ratio of 100,000	120 dB difference of 100 dB

Ratios get messy and awkward; dBs are more convenient.

Talk   Tech

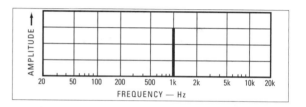

REVIEW OF LOGARITHMS

$100 = 10^2$ $\log 100 = 2$
$288 = 10^{2.4594}$ $\log 288 = 2.4594*$
$1000 = 10^3$ $\log 1000 = 3$

*from calculator

For example, let's listen to a 1000-Hz tone at a constant level:

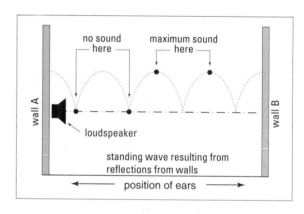

When these tones are reproduced on a loud-speaker, you will notice that changes in head position change the loudness of the sound due to room effects. For this reason, keep your head in one position during each test. Of course, if you are listening on headphones, room acoustics have no effect.

A change of level of 10 dB sounds like this:

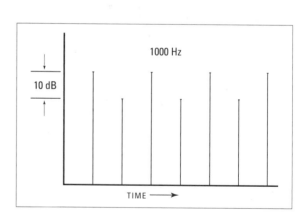

Talk   Tech

A change of 10 dB is often considered to be a doubling of loudness, or cutting loudness in half.

This is a 5-dB change of level:

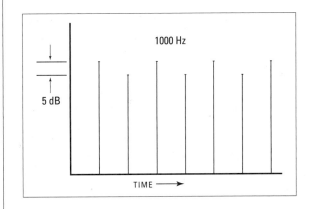

It may be difficult at first to detect a change of 2 dB. Try it. Changes will be made at the same five-second intervals:

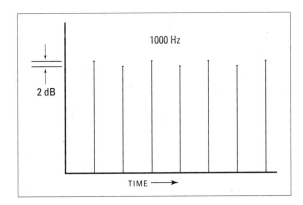

A change of 2 dB is easier to detect in louder sounds. Let's repeat the 2-dB change at a 10 dB higher level:

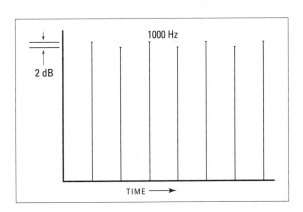

Talk   **Tech**

So, we see that the minimum detectable level change depends on the loudness of the 1000-Hz tone. That's not all. The loudness change also depends on frequency. Here is a repeat of the 10-dB change in level at 1000 Hz:

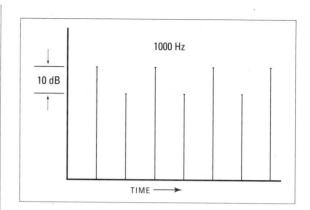

This is a 10-dB change in level at 100 Hz:

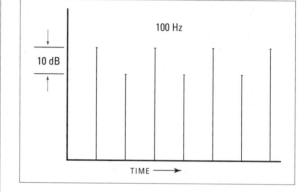

A 10-dB change in level is less noticeable at 100 Hz but very prominent at 1000 Hz. The minimum discernible level change depends both on the frequency and the level of the sound.

Now, music and speech cover a wide range of frequencies. A change in average level of 10 dB sounds like this in speech:

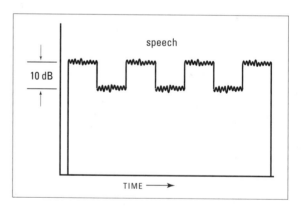

Talk   Tech

And now a 10-dB change in music:

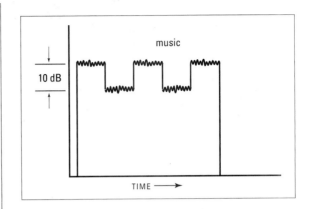

A change in level of 5 dB sounds like this in speech:

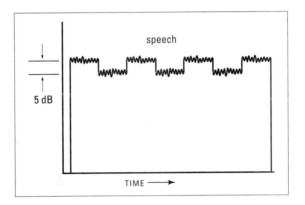

Now, a 5-dB change in music:

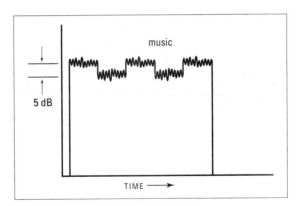

Talk   Tech

Here are changes in level of only 2 dB:

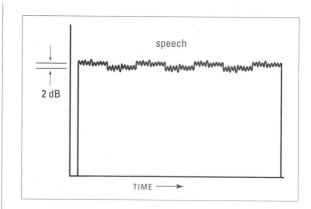

We can conclude that for ordinary speech
and music signals, a change in level of 2 dB is
about the smallest detectable by ear. We have
also learned what level changes of 5 and 10 dB
sound like.

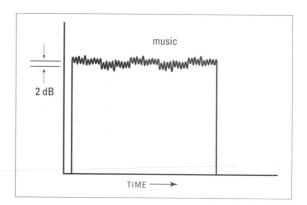

Let's test this new ability. The following speech
sounds will begin and end at a standard reference
level, but in between there will be three other
levels. Estimate the change in dB up or down
from the reference level:

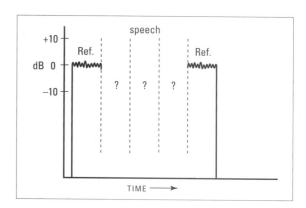

Talk   Tech

The first change was 10 dB down; then no change from the reference level; and finally, 10 dB up. How do your level judgments compare?

Let's repeat the speech sound for three different changes, again opening and closing with the reference level, with three unknowns in between.

This is more difficult. The changes were 4 dB up, 8 dB up, and 12 dB up. How do your judgments compare?

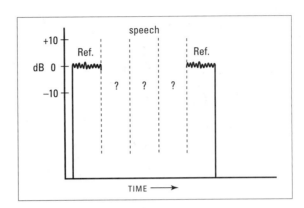

Now, let's exercise our judgment with music. Again, we will open and close with the reference level and present three level changes in between:

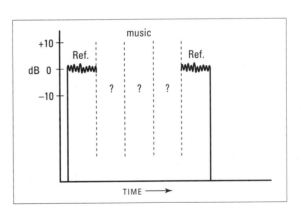

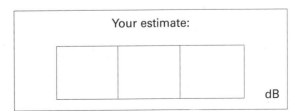

These changes were: first, 5 dB below reference; second, 5 dB above reference; and third, 10 dB below reference.

Here is another exercise in music using the same opening and closing reference levels:

The three changes this time were: 5 dB down, no change, and 5 dB up.

This is the end of this section, but go back over these exercises for further practice.

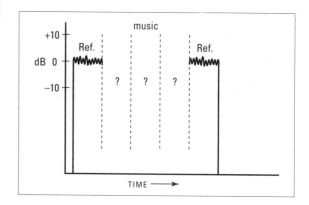

Estimating Frequency Band Limitations
Music, male and female voices

In this exercise, the width of the overall spectrum of the signal is altered in an orderly fashion so that we may hear the contributions of the various parts of the frequency spectrum.

First, we listen to music with full bandwidth:

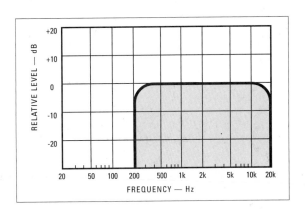

Now, let's see how the same music sounds with everything cut off below 200 Hz:

And now we will cut off everything below 500 Hz:

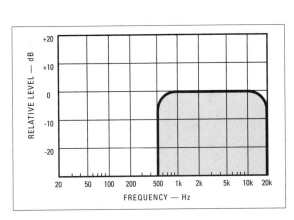

Talk   Tech

Cutting off everything below 1000 Hz has this effect on the music:

We see that an orchestra generates very significant amounts of energy in the low-frequency range and that the quality of the music suffers markedly if the full low-frequency range is restricted.

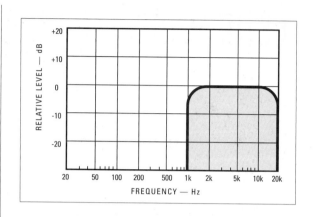

As a review, the following selections present the wide band and then the cutting off of signal components below 200, 500, and 1000 Hz, and then back to the reference wide-band condition. First, the reference wide-band condition:

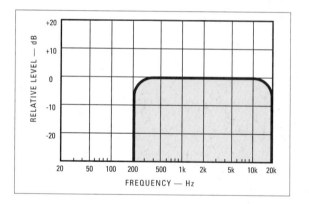

200 Hz lo-cut:

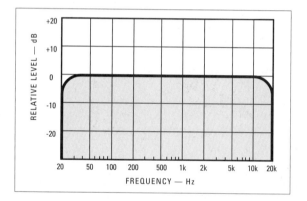

500 Hz lo-cut:

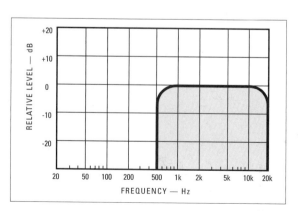

1000 Hz lo-cut:

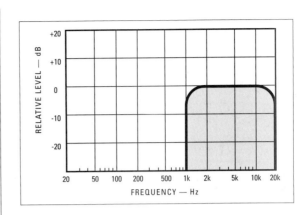

Back to the full-reference band:

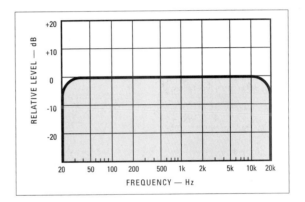

We have formed a general idea of the relative contribution of the lower frequencies to music quality. Now, let's explore the higher frequencies of the same musical selection. First, for reference, the full band again:

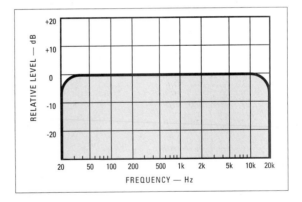

Now the energy above 8000 Hz will be cut off:

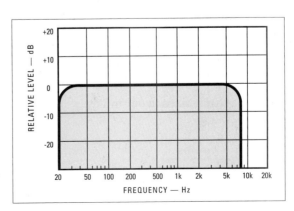

Cutting off everything above 5000 Hz:

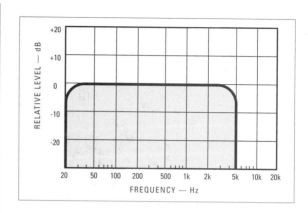

Cutting off everything above 2000 Hz:

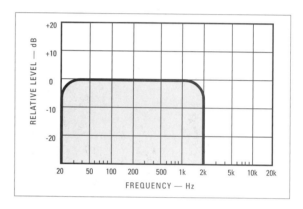

And now back to the reference full-band condition:

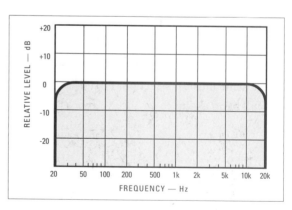

The quality of the music is also severely degraded when high-frequency components are lost. We will now review the previous hi-cut selections. We must always keep the full-band reference condition firmly fixed in our minds:

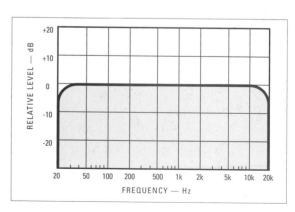

Talk   Tech

Now, the 8000-Hz hi-cut condition:

5000 Hz hi-cut:

2000 Hz hi-cut:

Back to the full-band reference condition:

The sound of the various instruments of the orchestra range, more or less, over the entire 20 Hz to 20,000 Hz audio spectrum. The human voice, on the other hand, covers a narrower range. In the following selections, we shall study the effect on a male voice of removing low-frequency energy. First, let's become familiar with the quality of this male voice with the full 20 Hz to 20,000 Hz band:

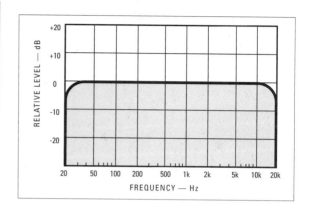

In this selection, low-frequency energy below 200 Hz is cut off:

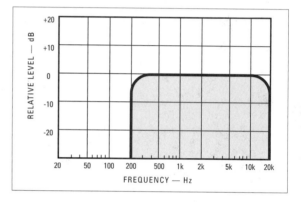

Next, everything below 500 Hz is removed:

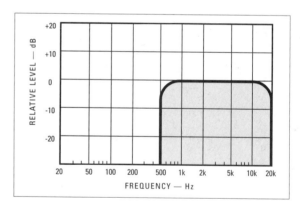

Now, everything below 1000 Hz will be cut off:

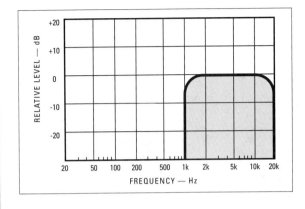

Going back to the full band:

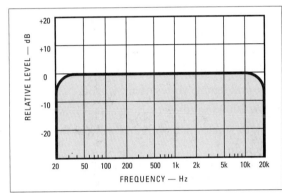

We shall now study the effect of removing high-frequency energy from the male voice. First, everything above 8000 Hz will be cut off:

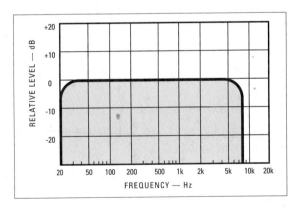

Next, everything above 5000 Hz will be removed:

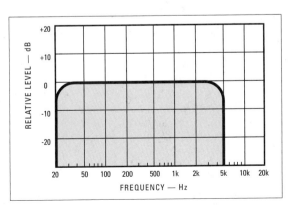

Talk   Tech

Now, everything above 2000 Hz will be cut off:

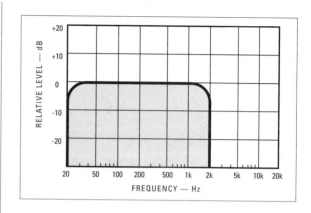

In real-life situations, both low- and high-frequency band limitations commonly occur together. We shall now hear the effect on both male and female voices of cutting off everything below 200 Hz and everything above 5000 Hz. First, the male voice with and without the limitation:

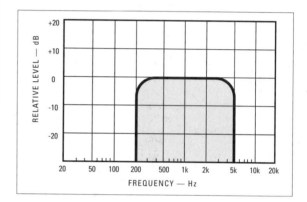

And now a female voice with and without the limitation:

The effect is surely apparent, but voice quality is not degraded too seriously by restricting the band to 200 Hz to 5000 Hz.

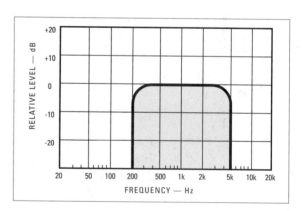

Talk   Tech

Narrowing the band even further, from 300 Hz on the low-frequency end to 3000 Hz on the high-frequency end, a telephone-like quality results:

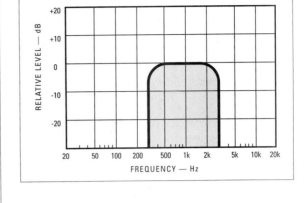

Even though the voice quality has greatly changed, it is interesting to note that the voices are recognizable and the words are quite understandable.

We have seen the effect on sound quality of limiting the pass band of an audio system. Next, we will have an exercise in estimating the degree of low- or high-frequency limitation in the following selections. In each case, the first selection is the wide band:

Lo-cut?	Hi-cut?
_____ Hz	_____ Hz

Did you detect a difference? The only limitation in the second selection was cutting off everything above 5000 Hz.

Try this one:

Lo-cut?	Hi-cut?
_____ Hz	_____ Hz

In this case, the high frequencies were not limited, but the low frequencies were cut off below 300 Hz.

Talk

Tech

A small radio receiver tuned to an AM station might pass something like a band from 300 Hz to 5000 Hz. Coming through this radio the music would sound like this compared to the full-band reference signal which precedes and follows it:

For practice, run back over this section until you readily detect low- and high-frequency deficiencies of the familiar sounds. This is a good start toward doing the same on unfamiliar sounds for which your only reference is your memory.

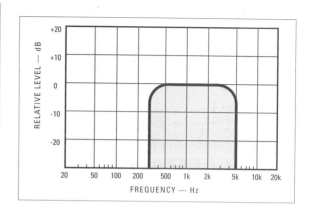

Frequency Response Irregularities
Their effect on music and speech

Talk   **Tech**

In previous lessons, we have heard the effect of cutting off high frequencies and cutting off low frequencies and limiting the band by cutting off both lows and highs. In those tests, we always returned to the flat, wide-band condition as our reference point. This wide-band flat response is our ideal. However, there are things which introduce irregularities into the flat response. In this lesson, we shall again use the flat, wide-band response as our point of departure and critically observe the effects of introducing irregularities of known magnitude and at known frequency. This can be done simply by adjusting an equalizer.

Here is our wide-band, flat response for reference:

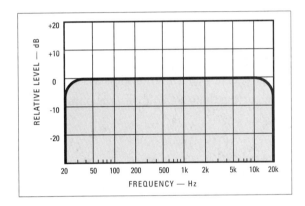

Now, we shall introduce a 10-dB peak centered at 8000 Hz:

This 10-dB peak at 8000 Hz also affects other frequency components both below and above 8000 Hz.

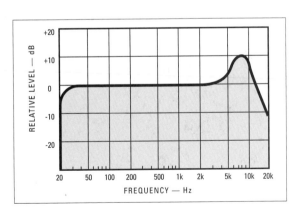

Talk

Tech

Next, we hear a 5-dB peak at 8000 Hz:

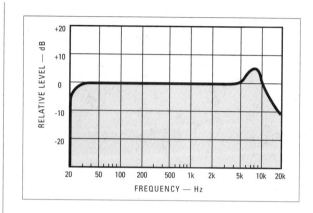

And now, back to the flat condition for reference:

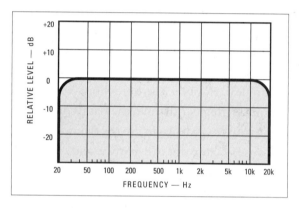

In Lesson 3, we heard the effect of cutting off low- and high-frequency portions of the audio spectrum. These we called *lo-cut* and *hi-cut*. Sometimes it is desirable to reduce low- and high-frequency contributions less drastically than cutting them off. For this, the phrase *roll-off* is used.

Talk   Tech

Rolling off the high frequencies a modest amount often makes the music sound better, less strident. Here is such an example:

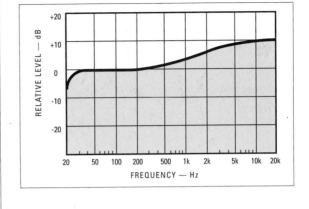

Now, gently rolling off the high frequencies above 5000 Hz:

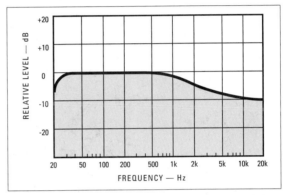

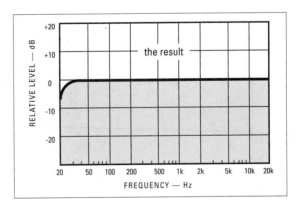

Rolling off the low-frequency energy may also improve the sound of music by minimizing a boomy effect, such as this selection:

Applying a low-frequency roll-off below 150 Hz has this effect:

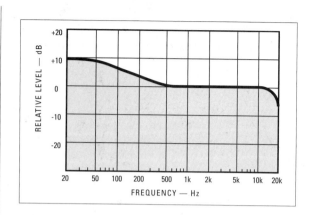

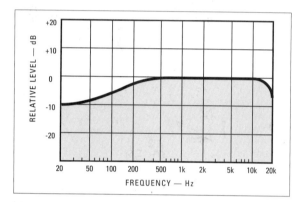

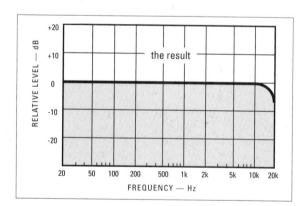

Now, let's see if you can identify the changes in the following five examples. All peaks and dips are of 10 dB magnitude and occur only at 150 Hz or 5000 Hz or both.

Here is Number 1:

Number 2:

Number 3:

Number 4:

Number 5:

Put your check mark where your estimate is:

No.	150 Hz Peak	150 Hz Dip	5 Hz Peak	5 Hz Dip
1				
2				
3				
4				
5				

It is easy to hear the difference, but deciding just what has happened is not as easy! Let's go through those five examples again but identifying the changes in response introduced.

First, Number 1. Number 1 has a 10-dB peak at 5000 Hz:

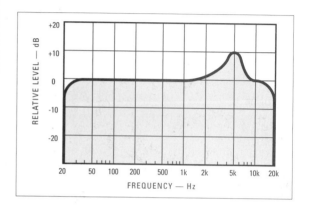

Next is Number 2. Number 2 has a 10-dB peak both at 150 Hz and 5000 Hz:

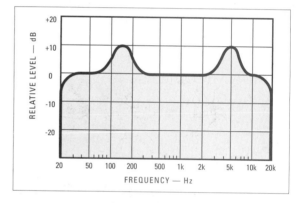

Now for Number 3. Number 3 has a 10-dB peak at 150 Hz and a dip at 5000 Hz:

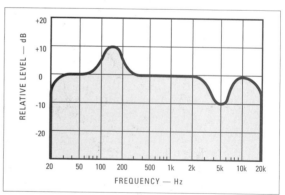

Number 4. Number 4 has a 10-dB dip at both 150 Hz and 5000 Hz:

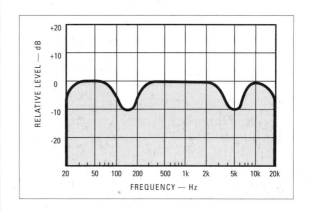

Now for the last one, Number 5. Number 5 has only a 10-dB peak at 150 Hz:

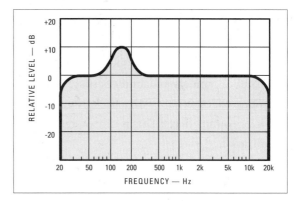

And now, back to the flat condition to restore our mental calibration:

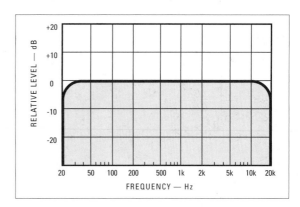

Response changes can occur anywhere in the audible band, either accidentally or on purpose. Let's consider one of these on-purpose cases. Equalization changes are often introduced to provide better understandability of speech. Listen critically to this speech sample, first with the flat condition:

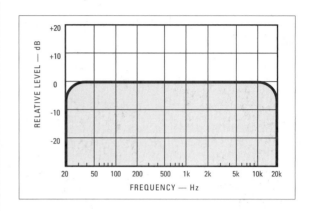

Now, notice carefully the effect of introducing a 5-dB boost at 3000 Hz:

Now, with a 10-dB boost at 3000 Hz:

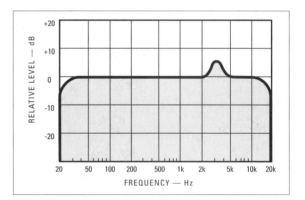

By boosting these important speech frequencies at 5 to 10 dB, understandability of speech can be improved, especially with a background of music or sound effects. This is called presence equalization.

In the following selection, we hear a mixture of voice and background music. The presence equalization at 3000 Hz is switched in and out. Note the improvement of understandability of the speech when the equalization is in:

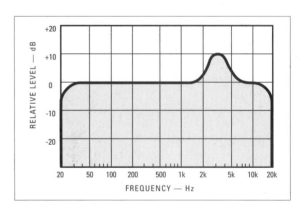

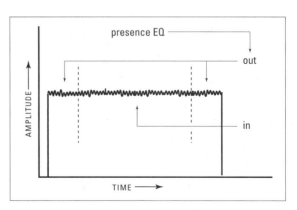

Clip-on microphones are very popular today, and most of them are capable of reasonably good quality if used properly. One problem with them is that the high-frequency components of the voice are quite directional, tending to miss the microphone. Boosting system response at the higher frequencies can compensate for this loss.

In the following selection, recorded with a clip-on microphone having flat response, notice the deficiency of high frequencies:

By introducing a 10-dB boost at 5000 Hz, the high-frequency components are restored:

Microphones clipped to shirt or necktie are very close to the chest and are prone to pick up chest resonances, which for a man, tend to overemphasize the voice components in the region of 700 to 800 Hz. We shall now hear once more the voice recorded with a clip-on microphone with the high-frequency boost intact, as before:

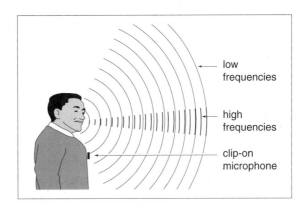

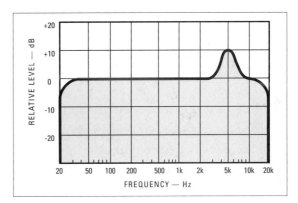

Now, to compensate for chest resonance, a dip of
6 dB at 750 Hz is introduced:

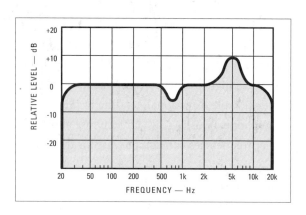

In the following selection, high-frequency and
chest resonance equalization will be switched
in and out together, so that the overall benefit
of such equalization on voice quality may be
appraised:

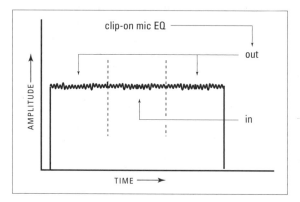

Thus, we see that intentional deviations from the
idealized flat response may actually yield better
recorded sound in the practical sense. Music may
be made more pleasing to the ear, and speech
may be made more understandable.

For review, go back over this lesson until you
can identify the approximate frequency at which
equalization irregularities occur and make a good
estimate of their magnitude.

Judgment of Sound Quality
Simple and complex sounds

Talk   **Tech**

Like everything else in life, some sounds may be described as simple, some as complex. Being able to distinguish between the simple and complex, both in the *kind* of difference and in the *amount* of difference, is a necessary skill for those in audio. In this exercise, we shall examine sounds of varying degrees of complexity, as we come to grips with that most nebulous aspect of sound—*sound quality*:

In previous lessons, we have called the sine wave an elemental and basic sound. All the energy of this simplest of all sounds is concentrated at a single frequency and, in the case of 1000 Hz, sounds like this:

If we change the sine wave shape to a triangular wave shape, it sounds different. Let's compare the 1000-Hz sine wave and the 1000-Hz triangular wave. Listen carefully for the differences in sound:

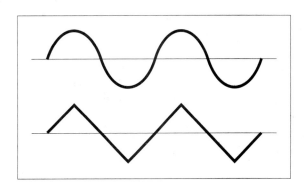

Talk   Tech

The triangular wave sounds different because of the harmonics it contains. Harmonics are multiples of the 1000-Hz fundamental. The sine wave has only the 1000-Hz fundamental, without any harmonics. The triangular wave has the 1000-Hz fundamental but also a weak third harmonic at 3000 Hz:

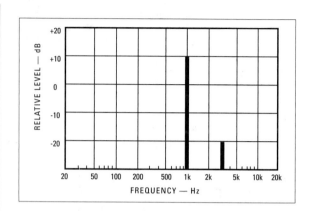

A fifth harmonic at 5000 Hz:

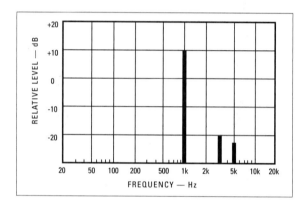

A seventh harmonic at 7000 Hz:

And so forth.

These harmonics are whole-number multiples of the fundamental frequency. In the case of the ideal triangular wave, only odd multiples are involved. Taken together, these harmonics account for the difference in sound between a sine wave and a triangular wave.

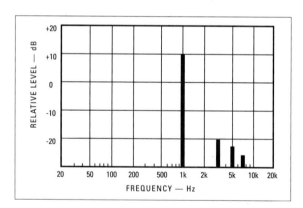

Talk   Tech

Let's refresh our memories on this difference between the 1000-Hz sine wave and the 1000-Hz triangular wave:

Remove the harmonics of the triangular wave and what do we have? For a little experiment, let's put the 1000-Hz triangular wave through a filter that rejects the harmonics but allows the fundamental to pass through:

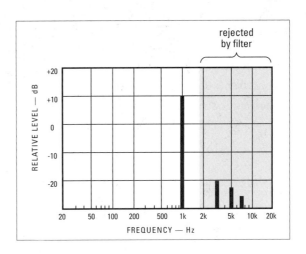

The 1000-Hz fundamental of the triangular wave is a simple sine wave!

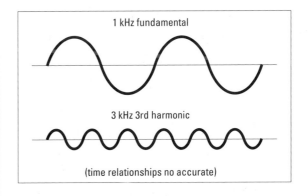

Now, let's use a different filter which rejects the fundamental so we can only hear the harmonics:

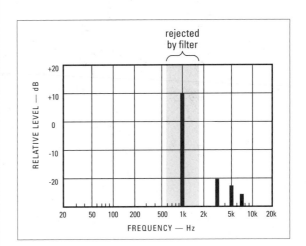

Talk   Tech

Even if it is not the most interesting sound in the world, we conclude that the triangular wave certainly has its own distinctive quality. The distinctiveness of its sound is all wrapped up in its harmonic structure. To emphasize this, let's review a bit. This is the simple 1000-Hz sine wave:

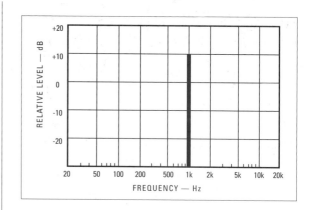

And this is the 1000-Hz triangular wave:

The harmonic content of a signal is the key to its distinctive sound quality.

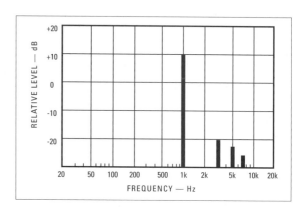

A 1000-Hz square wave has its own distinctive sound. All of its harmonics occur at the same odd multiples of the fundamental as with the triangular wave, but their magnitudes and time relationships are different. This is the sound of a 1000-Hz square wave:

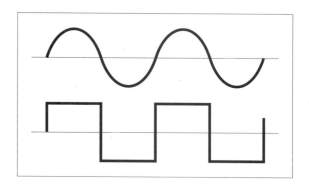

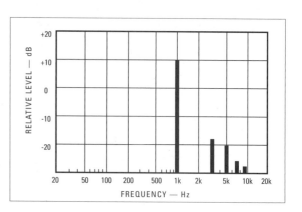

Here again, by use of filters, we can dissect the square wave. First, the harmonics are rejected, leaving only the sine fundamental:

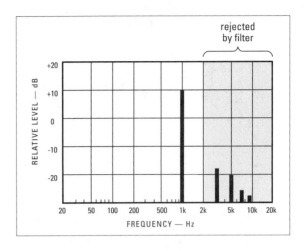

By filtering out the fundamental, only the low-level harmonics are left:

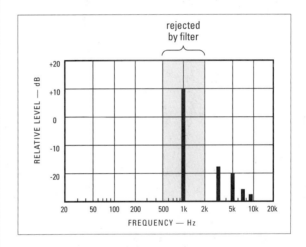

It is instructive to compare the triangular and square wave shapes and to identify the source of the differences with the harmonics. First, the triangular wave signal and its harmonics:

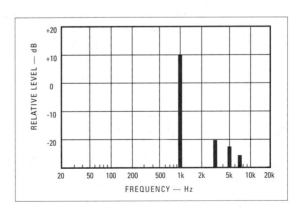

And now, the square wave signal and its harmonics:

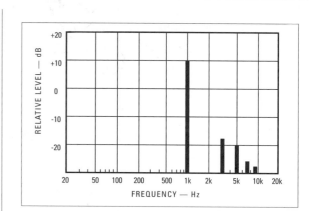

And now, only the harmonic contents of the triangular and square waves are compared:

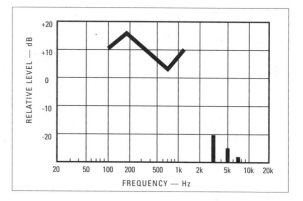

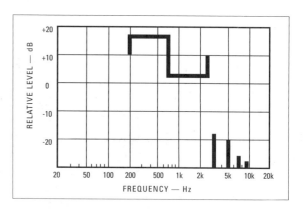

A violin playing middle C gives a fundamental frequency close to 260 Hz. Compare this violin tone with a pure sine wave at the same frequency from an oscillator:

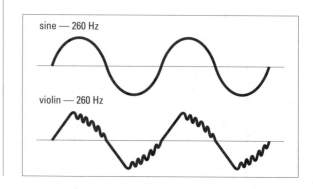

sine — 260 Hz

violin — 260 Hz

There is a richness to the violin tone which the sine wave certainly does not have. The violin tone is rich in overtones. As we deal with musical tones, it is fitting that we switch over to the musician's terminology. Instead of *harmonics*, the terms *overtones* or *partials* should be used. Later we shall see the logic behind this.

The violin tone can also be broken down into fundamental and overtones by means of filters. First, we shall hear the full tone, followed by the fundamental, and then the overtones:

Overtones dominate the violin sound. Its rich tonal quality depends entirely on the overtone pattern. The difference between the tone of a Stradivarius and a cheap violin lies principally in their different overtone patterns. The richer tone of the Stradivarius results from its richer overtone content.

Each instrument of the orchestra has its own overtone pattern, which gives it its characteristic sound. For example, middle C on the violin sounds quite different from the middle C on the piano:

This study of sound quality must place emphasis on the overtone structure. Therefore, let's compare the fundamentals and overtones of the violin and the piano:

To achieve high quality in the recording and reproduction of sound, it is necessary to preserve all the frequency components of that sound in their original form. Limitation of the frequency band or irregularities in frequency response, among other things, affect sound quality. This point can be demonstrated by going back to the middle C violin tone:

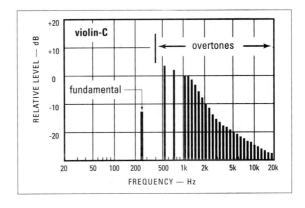

Middle C has a frequency of about 260 Hz. Overtones occur near 520, 780, 1040, and 1300 Hz, and up. If an equalizer peak of 10 dB is introduced at 1000 Hz, the original pattern of harmonics is changed and the overall sound is changed:

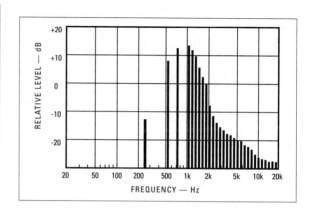

Also, if the higher frequency overtones of the violin are cut off by limiting the band, the quality of the tone is affected:

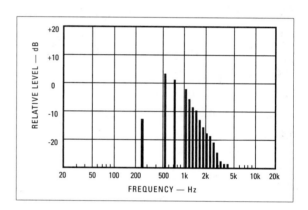

Some musical instruments have overtones that are not whole-number multiples of the fundamental and thus cannot be called harmonics. For such instruments, the general word *overtones* must be used. Piano tones, for example, are not strictly harmonic:

Bells produce a wild mixture of overtones and the fundamental may not even be recognized as such:

The overtones of drums are also not harmonically related to the fundamental, but they are responsible for the unique, rich drum sound:

Summarizing, we have learned that preserving the integrity of the fundamental and overtone pattern of our signal preserves the quality of the signal, and this is what high fidelity is all about.

Detecting Distortion
What it is and how it sounds

Talk   **Tech**

The output of any audio system invariably differs from what went into it because of distortion generated within the system. Of the several types of distortion, we shall concentrate on that type which is called *non-linear distortion*, which is of great concern in the world of high fidelity. Any distortion results in new frequency components being generated within the equipment which do not rightfully belong to the signal.

If the input signal to an amplifier is increased, we expect a corresponding increase in output. The operating region over which this is true is rightly called the *linear region*.

Every audio system, however, has its upper limit. Trying to get 100 watts out of a 10-watt amplifier certainly results in penetration of what is called the *non-linear region*. Our first exercise explores the distortion resulting from what is called *signal clipping*.

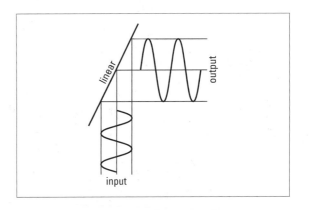

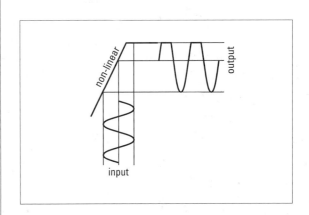

Talk   Tech

First, for orientation, we listen once more to a pure, undistorted 1000-Hz tone:

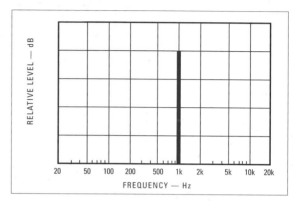

All the energy of this tone is concentrated at one point in the frequency spectrum. Practically speaking, there are no harmonics.

By increasing the amplitude, the signal is made to penetrate the non-linear region of the system. This clips the top off what was a nice symmetrical sine wave. The following effects are obtained by driving an amplifier into its non-linear region. For reference, the pure sine wave is included:

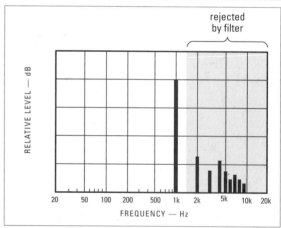

The change in sound of the clipped signal is the result of new frequencies, which have been generated by the non-linearity of the system. This is now a distorted sine wave. The new frequencies are harmonics, multiples of 1000 Hz. The distorted tone still has a strong 1000-Hz fundamental. We can prove this by inserting a filter in the circuit which rejects the harmonics and lets the 1000-Hz fundamental pass through:

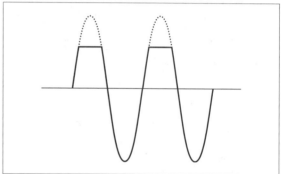

Now, let's look closer at the harmonics generated by the clipping. By inserting a different filter, the 1000-Hz fundamental is rejected, allowing us to focus attention on the harmonics:

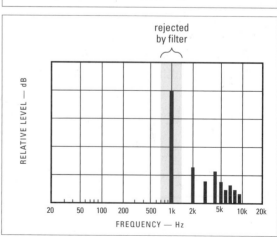

Talk   Tech

The harmonics of the clipped 1000-Hz wave occur at 2000 Hz, 3000 Hz, and 4000 Hz, and so on—all multiples of the 1000 Hz-fundamental.

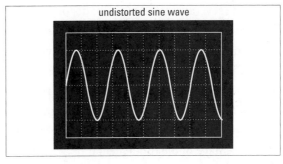
undistorted sine wave

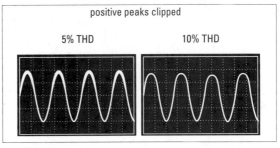
positive peaks clipped

5% THD   10% THD

This is what the harmonics look like on the cathode ray oscilloscope to the same scale as above.

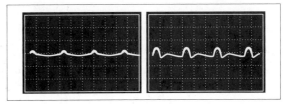

In balanced circuits, the signal may very well be clipped on both positive and negative excursions in a symmetrical fashion. The 1000-Hz sine wave clipped on both positive and negative peaks sounds like this:

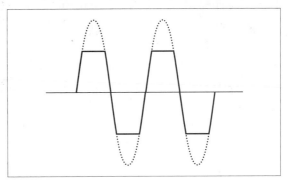

Harmonics generated by symmetrical clipping still occur at multiples of 1000 Hz, but the odd harmonics dominate.

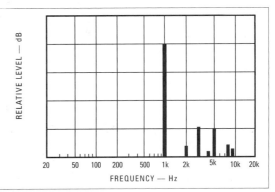

Talk

Tech

There are several ways to measure distortion of an audio system, but we shall concentrate on the one that is easiest to understand, even though it may not be the best. The simplest way to describe the amount of distortion is to filter out the fundamental and measure the harmonics remaining. These harmonics are then expressed as a percentage of the fundamental.

THD = Total harmonic distortion

$$\text{THD in \%} = \sqrt{\frac{\text{Sum of (harmonics}^2)}{\text{Fundamental}}} \times 100$$

To satisfy the mathematically inclined

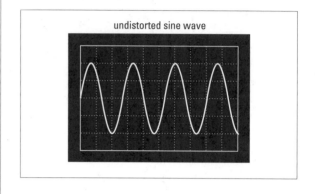

undistorted sine wave

To calibrate our judgment of distortion, we shall listen to the 1000-Hz sine wave clipped at various amounts. Ten percent harmonic distortion is considered to be very heavy distortion. The 1000-Hz sine wave clipped symmetrically to produce 10 percent total harmonic distortion sounds like this:

Reduced to 5 percent total harmonic distortion, the 1000-Hz clipped sine wave sounds somewhat more pure:

2 percent total harmonic distortion:

1 percent total harmonic distortion:

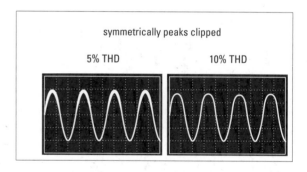

symmetrically peaks clipped

5% THD   10% THD

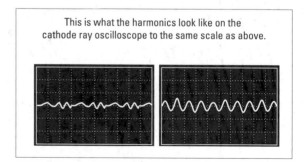

This is what the harmonics look like on the cathode ray oscilloscope to the same scale as above.

We shall now hear the 10, 5, 2, and 1 percent total harmonic distortion in succession:

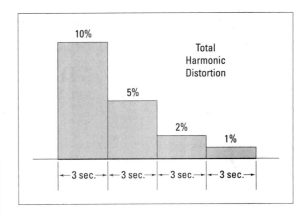

Five percent total harmonic distortion of a sine wave is reasonably discernible, but the 2 percent and 1 percent distortions are less noticeable. This much distortion in the case of music, however, may be more noticeable.

It is well for us to note at this point that modern professional power amplifiers and the better high-fidelity, consumer-type amplifiers are commonly rated as low as a few hundredths of 1 percent total harmonic distortion.

Clipping seriously distorts music and speech. In the following selection of music, the distortion is very low if your reproducing equipment is of high quality:

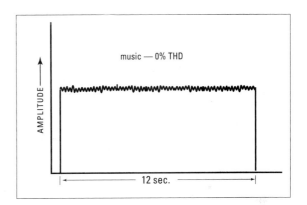

Now, we shall clip the signal symmetrically so that the total harmonic distortion is about 10 percent:

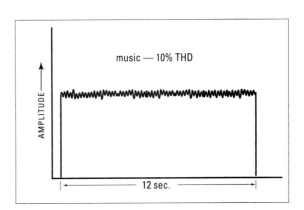

Next, the same signal with less clipping, a total harmonic distortion of 5 percent:

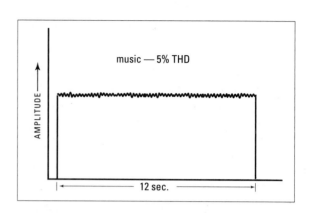

Can you detect a distortion of only 2 percent in this selection?:

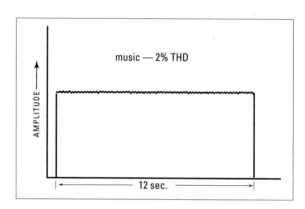

We now return to the clean music for reference:

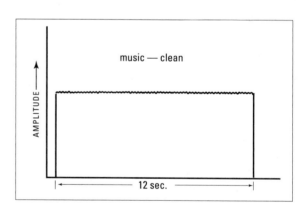

In the following musical selection, 2 percent distortion will be switched in and out at five-second intervals. The opening and closing portions are without the distortion:

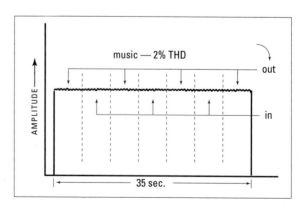

Talk   Tech

Harmonic distortion also degrades speech quality. The following selection will serve as our clean speech reference:

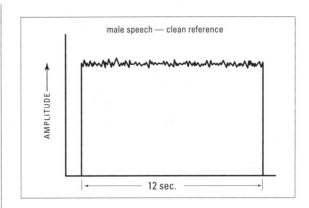

Clipping the signal symmetrically to the extent of 10 percent total harmonic distortion has this effect on speech:

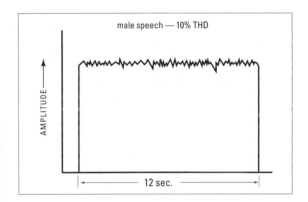

We now reduce the distortion to 5 percent:

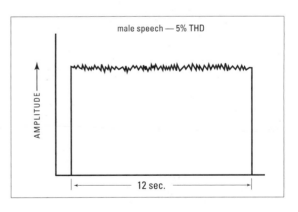

We shall now hear an A-B comparison between the clean speech and speech distorted to the extent of 2 percent total harmonic distortion. Let's see if you can detect this modest amount of distortion in speech:

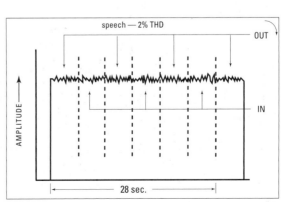

Is 2 percent total harmonic distortion easier or more difficult to detect in speech as compared to music?

A modified form of clipping results from applying too high a signal to a magnetic recorder.

This results in what is often called a *soft* type of clipping as the tape becomes saturated magnetically.

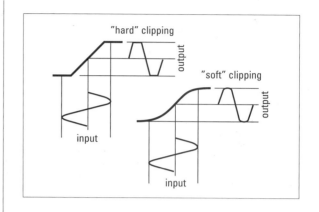

First, let us re-establish our reference by listening to the music selection with the VU meter of the recorder peaking at about zero in the normal way:

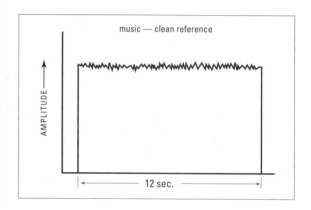

The only change made in the following example is that the input signal to the magnetic recorder under test is increased to overdrive it about 12 dB. Of course, the level you hear has been re-adjusted:

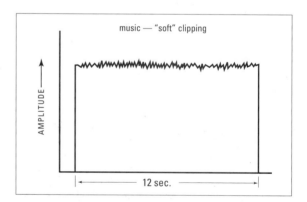

Talk   Tech

Another form of distortion has to do with the slight variations in the speed of the tape in a magnetic recorder or the rotational speed of the turntable as a disk recording is being played. Such speed changes result in unnatural shifts in frequency.

This can be dramatically demonstrated by the sound of the following 1000-Hz tone as we intentionally alter the speed of the drive system by applying finger pressure:

This illustrates what is commonly (and understandably) called wow.

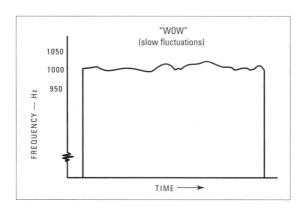

A similar form of distortion resulting from rapid speed fluctuations is called *flutter*. It can be caused, among other things, by dirty recording heads in magnetic recorders. Here is a 2500-Hz tone with serious flutter:

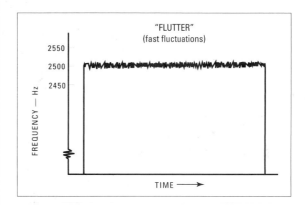

These variable-speed effects can seriously reduce the quality of music or speech reproduction. In the following music and speech selections, see if you can distinguish between clean passages and those marred by wow and flutter:

In summary, this section has demonstrated a few of the many forms of distortion and what they sound like. Distortion can so easily creep into our recording and reproducing systems. Critical listening can alert one to such faults.

Program material	Clean	Wow	Flutter
Music #1			
Music #2			
Music #3			
Speech #1			
Speech #2			
Speech #3			
Speech #4			

Reverberation Effects

On speech and music

Talk

Tech

Reverberation may be either friend or enemy; it can improve our program material or degrade it. Because we normally are not conscious of reverberation as a separate entity, it is well that we pause to dissect and define it.

Too much reverberation has this effect on speech:

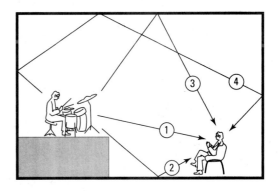

If reverberation is almost totally eliminated, the same speech is understandable, but it sounds rather "dry" and uninteresting:

Too little reverberation is as unpleasant and unnatural as too much.

Component:	
#1	Gets there first
#2	Gets there a little later
#3	Gets there still later
#4	Gets there much later and so on for thousands of other components

Such is the stuff of REVERBERATION.

Reverberation is a direct result of the relatively slow speed at which sound is propagated. The speed of sound is 1130 feet per second, or about 770 miles an hour. But even at this speed, it might take a tenth of a second to travel the length of a music hall. Some sound energy is lost at each reflection and it might take several seconds for successive bounces to reduce the level of the sound to inaudibility. In other words, in a confined space, it takes a little time for the sound to die away.

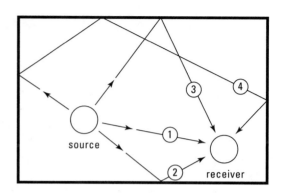

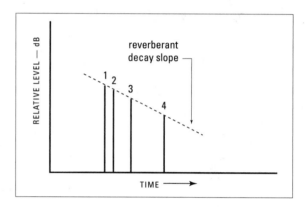

Talk   **Tech**

Reverberation time is, roughly, the time it takes a very loud sound to die away until it cannot be heard anymore. To be more precise and scientific about it, reverberation time is defined as that time it takes a sound suddenly cut off to decay 60 dB.

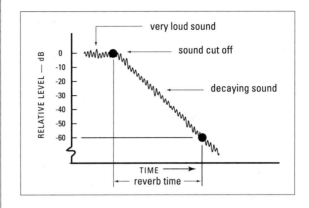

In the following example, the reverberation time is three seconds:

In the next example, the reverberation time is close to zero, and at the end of every syllable, the sound just stops:

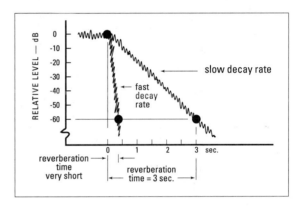

Talk   **Tech**

Between the extremes of too much and too little reverberation, we would expect to find some optimum reverberation time.

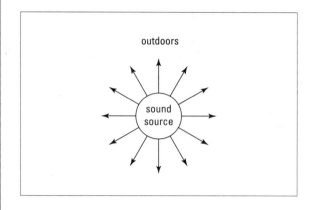

If an orchestra were to play outdoors, its sound would tend to be thin and dry. The same orchestra playing in a hall having a reverberation time of about one second sounds natural and pleasing, like this:

In the following selection, the reverberation time has been increased to simulate that of a hall having a reverberation time of 2½ seconds. Note how some of the musical details are blurred:

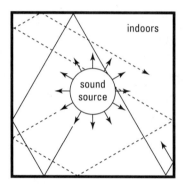

Increasing the reverberation time once more to 3½ seconds, the quality of the music is degraded even further:

And now, for comparison, we go back to the original selection:

We conclude that the reverberation time of the original selection, about one second, is close to optimum for this particular type of music.

The quality of speech is also greatly affected by the amount of reverberation present. We shall repeat the speech sample without reverberation heard earlier in this lesson:

With a reverberation time of 3½ seconds, the same speech selection sounds like this:

This is the way amplified speech might sound in a large cathedral. Both extremes yield unpleasant speech quality. Let's explore the effect of reverberation on speech in between these two extremes. This is with a reverberation time of one half second:

With a reverberation time of 1½ seconds the same speech sounds like this:

The understandability and naturalness of speech is actually better at shorter reverberation times.

As we listened to music, we found that excessive reverberation tended to blur the fine details of the various instruments. This is also true of speech. In the following exercise, the narrator is going to speak six one-syllable words with normal reverberation:

Let's analyze these words a bit. Note carefully that we depend upon the consonants at the end of each word to distinguish one word from another:

SIX LITTLE WORDS
(The intelligibility of speech is bound up in what happens to them.)

BAT-BAD-BACK-BASS-BAN-BATH

BA<u>T</u>

BA<u>D</u>

BA<u>CK</u>

BA<u>SS</u>

BA<u>N</u>

BA<u>TH</u>

Note also that the consonants are much softer than the opening parts of the word:

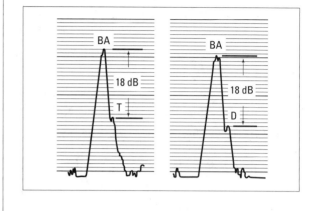

Anything that interferes with these low-level consonants reduces the intelligibility of the words. Reverberation is one thing but not the only thing that can seriously impair the understandability of speech by covering up these low-level consonants. Here is a repeat of the six one-syllable words with excessive reverberation, a reverberation time of 3½ seconds:

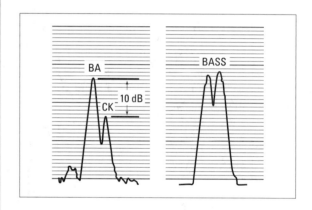

The slow trailing off of the sound of the first part of each word interferes with our hearing the consonants at the end of each word, and the identification of each word depends upon identifying this consonant.

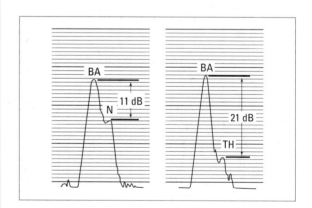

Talk   **Tech**

Let's explore in more detail the effect of reverberation on the intelligibility of these six single-syllable words.

With 3½ seconds reverberation time, the reverberation from the "BA..." covers the "..T."

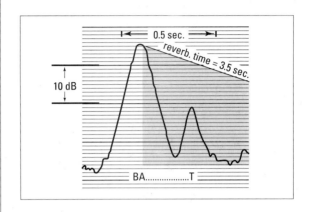

We have noted that a reverberation time of 3½ seconds is excessive; let's cut it to 2½ seconds:

This much reverberation still masks the important ending consonants.

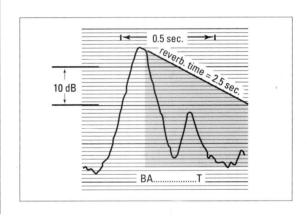

Now we will cut the reverberation time to 1½ seconds:

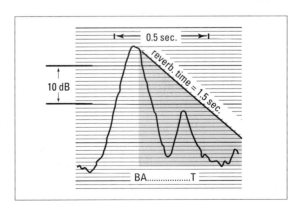

With 1½ seconds reverberation time, the "..T" is still covered.

Talk

Tech

The words are much more intelligible with 1½ seconds reverberation time. But now let's reduce it to one half second:

A half second is even better than 1½ seconds. The masking of the consonants is minimal with a reverberation time of one half second.

Reverberation affects female speech just as it does male speech. Here are two examples of female speech with acceptable and unacceptable amounts of reverberation:

Reverberation is very much a part of our enjoyment of music and our understanding of speech. It affects the quality of both speech and music, but it is very important to have the right amount.

The previous exercises were based on six one-syllable words with consonants at the end which helped us to understand why reverberation affects the intelligibility of speech. How about normal speech? Here is the way connected discourse sounds with a reverberation time of one half second, which we found acceptable for one syllable words:

Normal speech suffers, however, with a reverberation time of 2½ seconds:

Normal speech is slightly easier to comprehend in the presence of excessive reverberation than are isolated nonsense words or phrases. The context, the sense of the passage, helps us to guess at some of the lost portions. However, excessive reverberation tends to degrade all types of speech, even as it does music.

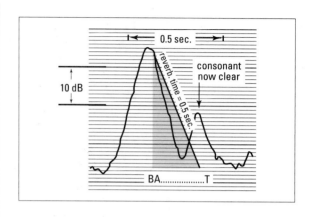

With ½ second reverberation time, the consonant "..T" is in the clear.

Signal Versus Noise

Their interrelationship

Talk

The program material we are interested in listening to or recording we shall call the *signal*. Any sound that interferes with enjoyment or comprehension of the signal is called *noise*. If the signal dominates, excellent. But if noise dominates, the signal is useless.

The relative strength of the signal compared to that of the noise is a very important factor in all communication systems. We even have a name for it: the *signal-to-noise ratio*. If the desired signal dominates, the signal-to-noise ratio is high, and all is well.

To get specific, let us designate the following musical selection as our signal:

It will be convenient for us to use white noise to interfere with our signal. White noise sounds like this:

Tech

SIGNAL...desired
NOISE...undesired

$$\frac{S}{N} \text{ ratio} = \frac{\text{Signal}}{\text{Noise}}$$

We wish to maximize the ratio by:
increasing signal level
or
decreasing noise level
or
both

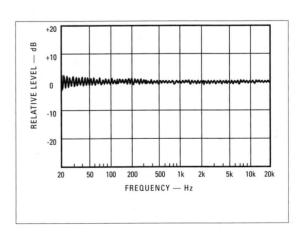

Now, we shall mix the signal and the white noise at equal levels:

The signal is almost completely buried in noise, an obviously unworkable condition. In this case, we have a signal-to-noise ratio of one to one. This is commonly referred to as a signal-to-noise ratio of zero dB. That is, the signal level and the noise level are separated by zero dB.

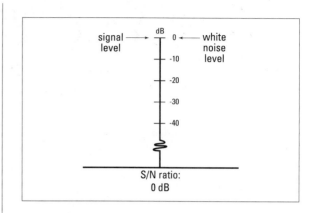

To improve the situation, the noise is reduced to a level 10 dB below that of the signal. The signal-to-noise ratio of the following selection is thus 10 dB:

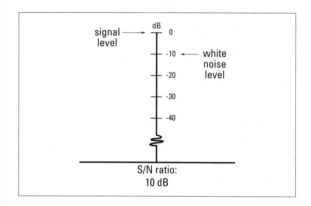

With a signal-to-noise ratio of 20 dB, our music signal really begins to emerge:

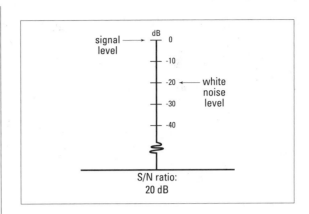

A signal-to-noise ratio of 30 dB sounds like this:

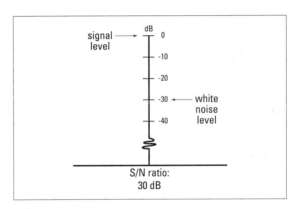

Talk   Tech

The following is a signal-to-noise ratio of 40 dB:

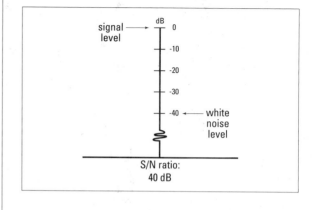

At a signal-to-noise ratio of 40 dB, it becomes more difficult to hear the noise.

In the following selection, the white noise is first injected at a level 40 dB below the music and increased in 10 dB steps. During the first five seconds, however, only the noise of the reproducing system prevails. Can you hear it?:

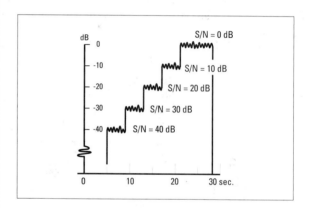

Noise interferes with speech as well as music. In a previous lesson, we saw how reverberation can reduce intelligibility of speech by masking the all-important consonants. Reverberation is a kind of noise, so we can expect white noise to affect the understandability of speech in a similar way. Let's use the same six single-syllable test words we used before:

A signal-to-noise ratio of 30 dB is produced by injecting white noise:

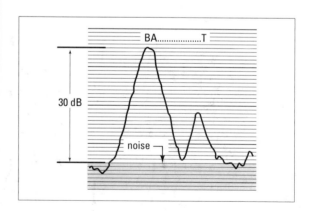

The speech is quite intelligible in spite of the random noise. Let's repeat this with a signal-to-noise ratio of 20 dB:

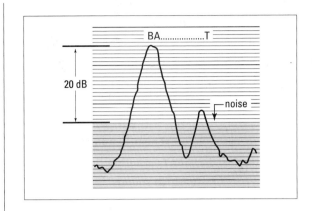

As the level of the consonants is about 20 dB below that of the rest of each word, a signal-to-noise ratio of 20 dB begins to take its toll in intelligibility. This is a signal-to-noise ratio of 15 dB:

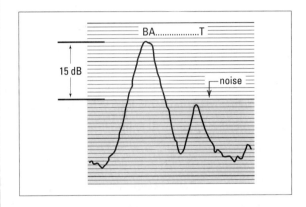

Next, a 10 dB signal-to-noise ratio really destroys intelligibility of the one-syllable words, because the noise covers the low-level consonants:

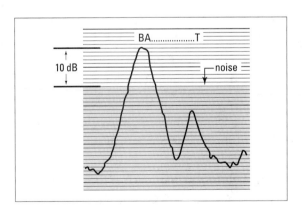

We are naturally well acquainted with music and speech signals. The inevitable noise that often interferes with the desired signal is less familiar to us. For this reason, let's focus our attention on some common sources of noise.

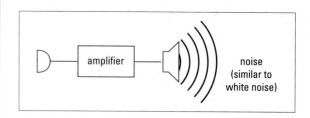

Every electrical circuit generates noise. In fact, electrons flowing in any circuit produce a characteristic noise which sounds like this:

Electrical current flowing in every transistor, every piece of wire, generates a hissing sound like we have just heard. Fortunately, it is quite weak, but certain circuit faults can make it a problem.

A very common noise is hum originating in the alternating current power source. The following sample of 60-Hz hum will sound familiar to all:

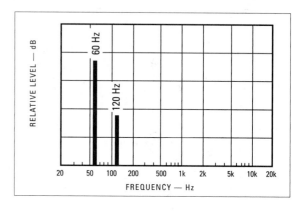

Many circuits create harmonics of 60 Hz and often what we call 60-Hz hum may actually be 120 Hz. This is a 60 Hz with harmonics:

s is a term describing the case of an undesired signal interfering with the desired signal. In this case, someone else's signal is noise to us! If the two signals are dissimilar, the interference is especially noticeable. In the following selection, it doesn't take much music to be heard during the pauses of speech:

Radio frequency signals, such as those from nearby radio and television broadcasting stations, can easily penetrate audio circuits if there is improper shielding. Here again, the next person's signal can be a noise problem to us:

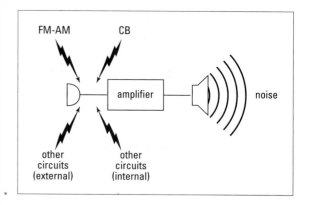

Although there are many other types of electrical noise, these are typical and illustrative.

Talk   **Tech**

There are also noises which get into electrical circuits by way of some sort of mechanical action.

Switching electrical circuits can produce clicks and pops if the switches are not carefully designed and built, and these noises can degrade the quality of a signal:

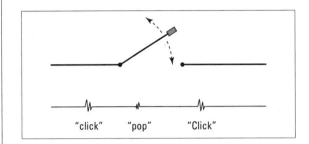

"click"   "pop"   "Click"

The noise of heating, ventilating, and air conditioning equipment is often of high enough level to degrade a recording or interfere with listening. This is usually the noise of motors or fans:

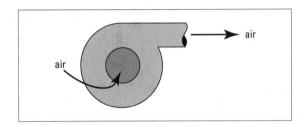

In listening to live or reproduced music or speech, signal quality can be affected by environmental noise. The mere presence of people in an audience results in noises of breathing, movement, coughing, rustling paper, and so forth:

If the audience is paying rapt attention, this noise is low. If restive, the noise increases greatly.

Listening to interesting program material tends to make one oblivious to all but very high noise levels. However, the person evaluating such program material must be objective and alert, consciously focusing attention on possible flaws such as excessive background noise.

Voice Colorations
How they sound and what causes them

 Talk   **Tech**

In previous lessons, we have noted the effect on the sound of a voice of peaks and dips in the response of an audio system. In this lesson, we shall concentrate on various acoustical effects which make a voice sound unnatural.

Unnatural voice sound	=	Voice coloration

In recording a voice in a room, there is no escaping the acoustical effect of the surroundings. The sound is contained by the surfaces of the room; and size, shape, and proportions of the room, and the absorbing and reflecting characteristics of the surfaces determine the sound field in the room. For example, my voice is being recorded in an acoustically treated studio with the microphone about six inches from my lips. At such a close distance, the room effects are certainly present but not dominant. Notice carefully the change in character of my voice as the microphone is placed at successively greater distances from me.

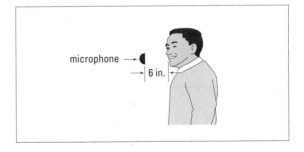

The microphone is now in its normal position, about six inches from my lips.

The microphone is now about three feet from me, but I am still talking in the same tone of voice as before.

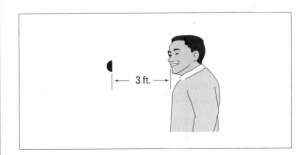

The microphone is now ten feet from me. You will notice a distinct change in voice quality as the distance is increased.

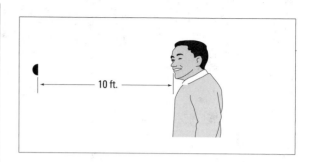

The microphone is now back to the three-foot distance, as you note carefully the change in voice quality as effected by the distance to the microphone.

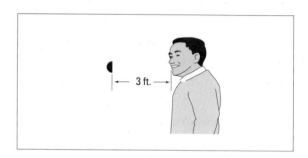

The microphone is now back in its normal position, about six inches from my lips.

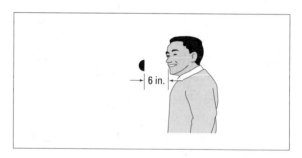

Talk

Tech

With the microphone close to my lips, the direct sound dominates. The sound reflected from the walls, floor, and ceiling is weaker because it travels farther and some sound energy is lost at each reflection. The greater the microphone distance, the more the room effect dominates.

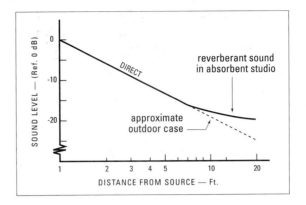

Now we shall go to another room, whose surfaces are largely hard and reflective, and repeat the experiment.

This room is untreated acoustically and is very "live." Even with the microphone at the normal six-inch distance, you can hear that my voice sounds distinctly different from that in the studio.

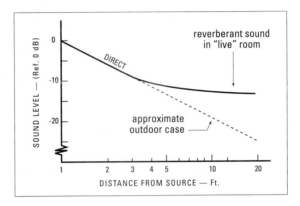

The microphone is now three feet from my lips. Notice that the reverberation of the room changes the sound of my voice materially.

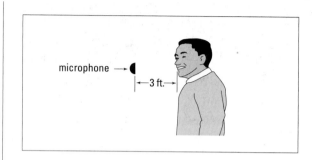

The microphone has now been moved so that it is ten feet from me. The direct sound is lower because of the distance and the reverberant sound is dominant.

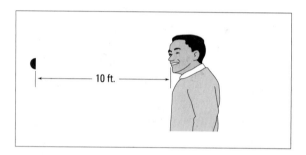

The microphone is now back to the three-foot distance, and you will again note the room effect.

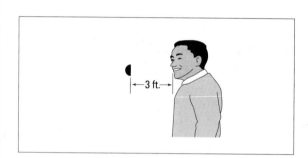

The microphone is now back at the normal six-inch distance. Although the room effect has decreased at this distance, it is still there.

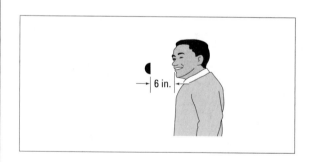

Talk

Tech

These two experiments focus our attention on the importance of room acoustics and microphone distance on recorded voice quality. However, further analysis is impractical because of the overwhelmingly complex nature of the sound field in a room. For this reason, we shall reduce the next experiment to the simple case of a single acoustical reflection from a sheet of plywood.

In this experiment, I will hold the microphone at a constant distance from my lips so that the direct sound will be unchanged.

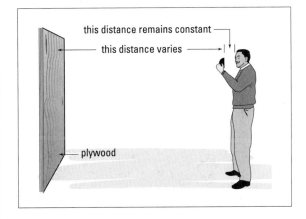

By walking toward the plywood, the sound reflected from it will increase the closer I get. Here we go!

I am now about ten feet from the plywood sheet and walking slowly toward it, talking continually so that you can detect any changes in the quality of my voice. Now I am about five feet from the plywood and still moving. Note carefully the change in my voice as I move closer to the plywood. Do you hear a changing roughness in my voice as the direct and reflected rays combine? As I now move slowly backward, my voice returns to normal.

The coloration of my voice while close to the plywood sheet is the result of the sound of my voice traveling directly to the microphone combining with the reflection from the plywood, which is slightly later because of the greater distance traveled. This time delay of the reflected ray is small (of the order of a thousandth of a second) but its influence is great.

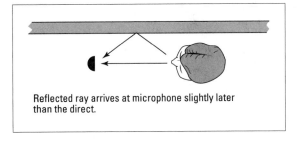

Reflected ray arrives at microphone slightly later than the direct.

Talk   Tech

The entire effect can be simulated for easy study by using a delay device. In the following example, a voice signal is combined with the same signal delayed one-half of a thousandth of a second (or one-half millisecond) with respect to the direct sound:

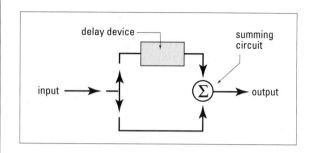

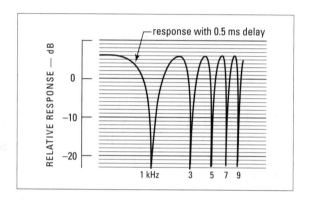

A one-millisecond delay affects the voice this way:

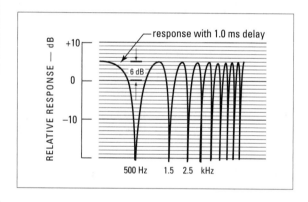

Increasing the delay to 1½ milliseconds has this effect on the voice:

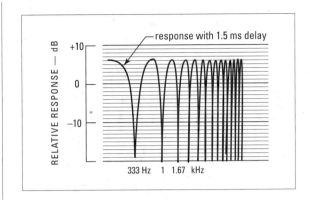

We now go back to the reference sound without the delayed reflection:

The effect of a delayed signal is most noticeable as the changes are taking place. The following example is similar to those we have just heard except that the delay varies continually between zero and 1½ milliseconds:

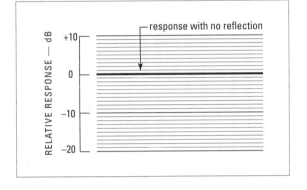

Voice colorations result any time a sound component is combined with itself delayed a bit. The plywood reflector provided such a delay with a single microphone. A hard table top close to the microphone can do the same thing.

Comb filter colorations
are generated
by these arrangements

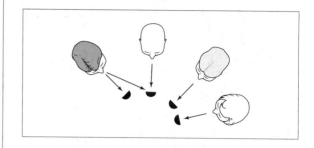

If the same sound strikes two microphones separated at a distance, and the outputs of the two are combined, wild frequency response variations will result. At frequencies at which the two components are in phase, the signals add, giving a 6-dB peak. At frequencies at which they are out of phase, they cancel, resulting in a 30- or 40-dB dip in response. Down through the audible spectrum, these peaks and dips drastically change our normally uniform response, and this is what changes the character of the sound. This is commonly called a comb filter because the frequency response peaks and dips look like a comb when plotted.

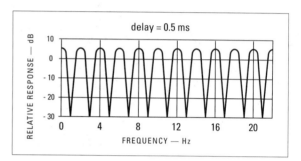

Critical evaluation of audio signals requires the ability to detect voice colorations and to form some idea of their cause. Some of the following selections are normal, recorded in a studio with a close microphone. Others are colored by one of the methods we have studied.

Talk

Tech

See if you can identify those with colorations and the source of the coloration:

Selection A:

Selection B:

Selection C:

Selection D:

Selection E:

Selection F:

Selection G:

Selection H:

Selection I:

Selection J:

Go back over the material in this lesson until you are familiar with the sound of voice colorations and can give a good estimate as to their probable causes.

Use evaluation sheet to record your identifications:

Voice Colorations Evaluation Sheet

Answers on page 89

COLORATION	MUSICAL SELECTION									
	A	B	C	D	E	F	G	H	I	J
Normal, uncolored (treated studio mic distance 6 in.)										
Treated studio mic distance 3 ft.										
Treated studio mic distance 10 ft.										
Live room mic distance 5 ft.										
Live room mic distance 10 in.										
Comb filter 0.5 millisecond delay										
Comb filter 1.0 millisecond delay										
Comb filter 1.5 millisecond delay										

Voice Colorations Evaluation Sheet

Answers

COLORATION	MUSICAL SELECTION									
	A	B	C	D	E	F	G	H	I	J
Normal, uncolored (treated studio mic distance 6 in.)		X			X				X	
Treated studio mic distance 3 ft.							X			
Treated studio mic distance 10 ft.										X
Live room mic distance 5 ft.			X							
Live room mic distance 10 in.								X		
Comb filter 0.5 millisecond delay	X									
Comb filter 1.0 millisecond delay				X						
Comb filter 1.5 millisecond delay						X				

Listening With Discernment
A review

Talk

Tech

This lesson concentrates on music. Ten different musical selections will be presented, each having a single dominant fault artificially induced.

The musical selections from one to two minutes in length are long enough to enable you to listen carefully, critically, and analytically. This approximates the real-life situations better than the brief speech and music selections of the previous lessons.

The object of the game is for you to concentrate on each musical selection, in your most discriminating way, to identify the dominant fault which has been introduced.

To help you maintain a proper reference, the opening and closing 20 seconds of each selection will be clean (without the fault). These 20-second sections will be marked by short breaks in the music.

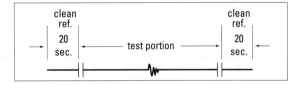

It is quite possible that you may detect one or more less dominant faults which may have been unintentionally introduced at some stage of the recording process or possibly introduced by your own reproducing equipment.

Talk

Tech

A form has been provided in the manual for you to jot down your identification of the artificially introduced dominant fault for each selection. If other faults are detected, record them at the bottom of the form in the space provided. Are you ready? All right, let's go!

First, Selection 1:

Selection 2:

Selection 3:

Selection 4:

Selection 5:

Selection 6:

Selection 7:

Selection 8:

Selection 9:

Selection 10:

That concludes both the Critical Listening course and Lesson 10. Maximum benefit can be derived from this course only by going back over each lesson until it is mastered.

See Supplemental Data for Listening With Discernment Evaluation Sheet on pages 95-97

Listening With Discernment Evaluation Sheet

Answers on page 94

INTENTIONAL FAULTS	MUSICAL SELECTION									
	1	2	3	4	5	6	7	8	9	10
Low frequencies cut off										
High frequencies cut off										
High-frequency peak										
Low-frequency peak										
Distortion: (clipping)										
Excessive reverberation										
High background noise										
UNINTENTIONAL FAULTS										
Hum										
Record scratch										
Wow										
Turntable rumble										
Flutter										
Dropouts										
Other										

Listening With Discernment Evaluation Sheet

Answers

INTENTIONAL FAULTS	MUSICAL SELECTION									
	1	2	3	4	5	6	7	8	9	10
Low frequencies cut off							X			
High frequencies cut off			X							X
High-frequency peak	X									
Low-frequency peak		X								
Distortion: (clipping)					X				X	
Excessive reverberation								X		
High background noise				X		X				
UNINTENTIONAL FAULTS										
Hum										
Record scratch										
Wow										
Turntable rumble										
Flutter										
Dropouts										
Other										

Supplemental Data for
Listening with Discernment Evaluation Sheet

Selection 1

The fault intentionally introduced in Musical Selection 1 is a high-frequency peak of 15 dB centered on 6 kHz.

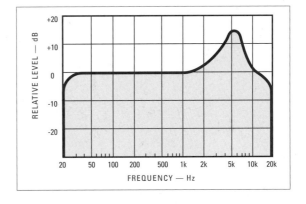

Selection 2

In Musical Selection 2, a 14-dB peak centered about 200 kHz has been introduced.

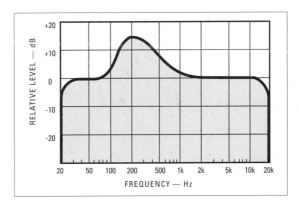

Selection 3

Musical Selection 3 has a drastic roll-off of high frequencies above 1 kHz.

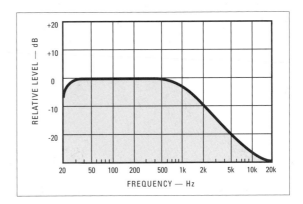

Talk   Tech

Selection 4

Musical Selection 4 has a high background noise. White noise has been introduced to give a signal-to-noise ratio of 25 dB.

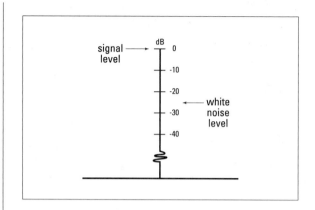

Selection 5

Musical Selection 5 has serious clipping on both positive and negative peaks.

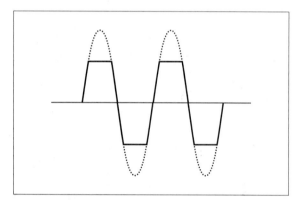

Selection 6

Musical Selection 6 has a high background noise level somewhat lower than that of Selection 4. The signal-to-noise ratio is 20 dB.

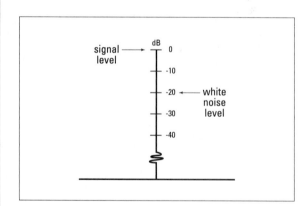

Selection 7

Musical Selection 7 has a drastic low-frequency roll-off below about 3 kHz.

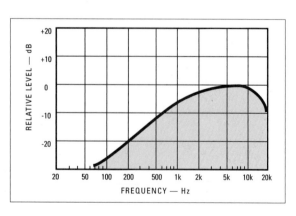

Selection 8

Excessive reverberation has been applied to
Musical Selection 8. The reverberation time of
the artificial reverberator is 2½ seconds with a 25-
millisecond delay applied to improve naturalness.

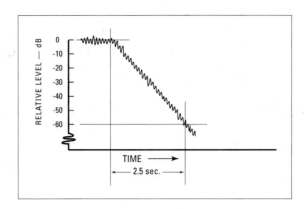

Selection 9

Musical Selection 9 suffers from the same serious
symmetrical clipping as Selection 5.

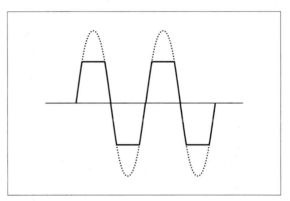

Selection 10

Selection 10 has the same high-frequency roll-off
above 1 kHz as Selection 3.

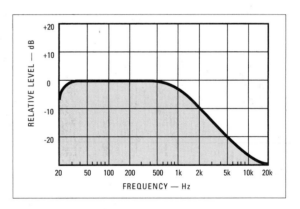

BOOK 2

Auditory Perception

Eight Units Designed for Instruction in the
Psychoacoustical Aspects of Human Hearing

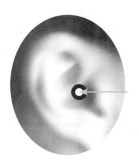

Introduction to the Structure and Function of the Human Hearing System

Anatomy of the Ear

It is difficult to consider the human ear without resorting to superlatives. The more one understands the human hearing system, the more awed one becomes. The ear/brain system truly is remarkable, and our understanding of it is fragmentary at best. However, what is known provides a basis of understanding that is of great value to the practicing musician, audio engineer, or high-fidelity enthusiast.

A simplified cross section of the ear is shown in Fig. 1. The pinna, or external ear, is far more than a decoration, as we shall see later. The sound gathered by the pinna enters the auditory canal (auditory meatus) and actuates the eardrum (tympanic membrane). The pinna, auditory canal, and the eardrum diaphragm constitute the outer ear.

The middle ear's only opening to the outside world is through the eustachian tube, which provides a rather tortuous path into the pharynx for the air flow necessary to equalize the static air pressure on the two sides of the eardrum. If this tube becomes clogged through infection, a cold, or a sudden change of altitude while riding in a light plane (commercial airplanes are pressurized), it can cause discomfort. The audio expert understands the eardrum as an "acoustic suspension" device working against the compliance of the air trapped in the middle ear. If both sides of the eardrum were exposed to the sound waves, its effect would be seriously diminished.

The three tiny bones of the middle ear, the malleus, incus, and stapes (or hammer, anvil, and stirrup in common terms), are a mechanical link between the eardrum and the oval window of the cochlea. We shall see later how this bony linkage provides a highly efficient transfer of sound energy from air to the liquid of the cochlea.

The cochlea is the inner ear. The cochlea is a mechanical-to-electrical transducer which translates vibratory energy to electrical impulses and sends them to the brain via the auditory nerve. The cochlea is coiled like a snail shell and is deeply embedded in the temporal bone. It is filled with fluid and contains membranes and hair cells that analyze the sound.

The Function of the Outer Ear

As mentioned above, the pinna has certain sound-gathering functions. Cupping the hand behind the ear augments this sound gathering and allows us to hear fainter sounds. In Fig. 2, the solid line shows the increase in sound pressure at the eardrum above that of the free, undisturbed sound field. The sound amplification, however, is the result of more than the sound-gathering effect of the pinna. The auditory canal acts something like an organ pipe closed at one end. When the length of such a pipe is one-fourth of the wavelength of the sound impinging on the open end, a significant rise in sound pressure results at the closed end. When the sound falling on the open end of the auditory canal is of such a frequency that the length of the canal is one-fourth wavelength, this increase in sound pressure occurs at the eardrum. From the solid curve of Fig. 2, we see that such a sound amplification approaches 20 dB in the region of 2000 Hz.

An interesting question is, "How much does it help to cup the hand behind the hear?" The

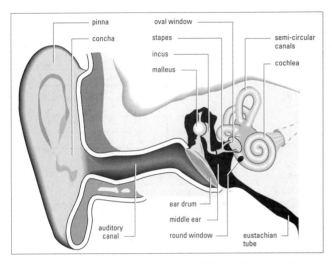

Figure 1 Illustration of the outer, middle, and inner ears in man

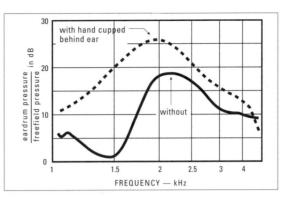

Figure 2 The sound pressure at the eardrum. Solid line: normal. Broken line: with hand cupped behind the pinna, which amounts to an enlargement of the pinna (after Weiner and Ross)

broken curve in Fig. 2 shows this condition. The difference between the two curves, the contribution of the cupped hand, varies from just a few dB at most frequencies to about 20 dB at 1500 Hz. This amount of gain obtained by cupping the hand behind the ear can mean the difference between understanding and not understanding speech for someone with impaired hearing.

We see, then, that the pinna, the auditory canal, and the eardrum constitute a complex acoustical cavity that increases the sound pressure at the eardrum. Diffraction of sound by the head also adds a bit to this amplification of sound pressure. The amount of the overall amplification varies with frequency, but its maximum occurs in the speech frequencies and amounts to about 20 dB (tenfold) at the peak.

Localization Cues From the Outer Ear

We principally depend upon differences in sound pressure level and timing for two-eared localization of sound sources, but is it possible to locate sound with only one ear? Through the years, the tendency has been to answer this question in the negative, but recent findings have given us a new appreciation of the importance of folds, ridges, and depressions of the pinna. Notice that they are asymmetric around the entrance to the auditory canal, called the *concha*. Sound coming from below, as in Fig. 3A, might be reflected from the top of the concha to the

point labeled "x," which we will take as the center of the opening of the auditory canal. The point of reflection is about half an inch from x, which means that the reflected component travels one inch farther than the component arriving directly at x. Because it takes sound 74 microseconds to travel one inch, the direct and the reflected components will combine at with a delay of 74 microseconds between them. Combining two signals this way results in peaks and nulls throughout the audible spectrum in what is called *comb filter* distortion, so called because the spectrum plotted on a linear frequency scale looks like a comb. The first null, or dip, occurs at a frequency of $1/(2t)$ in which "t" is the time delay between the two signals. For the 74 microsecond delay, this first dip falls in the audible spectrum at about 6800 Hz. In Fig. 3B, the center of the auditory canal opening can be taken as 0.375 inch from the concha wall, which results in a delay distance of $(2)(0.375 \text{ inch}) = 0.75$ inch. This translates, as above, to a delay of 55 microseconds. A delay of 55 microseconds gives a first dip at 9000 Hz. A similar approach to Fig. 3C, with its quarter inch spacing or half-inch delay distance, yields a dip at 13,500 Hz.

The asymmetry of the pinna around the entrance to the auditory canal yields a first minimum at a frequency dependent upon the angle of arrival of the sound. This seems to be the type of cue a single ear can use to interpret the direction to the source of a sound. This effect is demonstrated in Book 2's Unit 7.

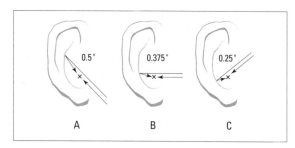

Figure 3 The pinna imposes special filtering on incoming sound through the interaction of direct sound with reflections from irregularities of the pinna. This "comb filtering" produces notches in the spectrum that are interpreted by the brain as directional cues (after Rodgers).

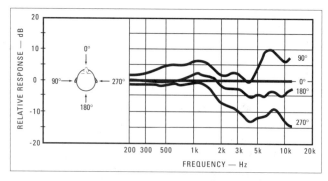

Figure 4 Variations of sound pressure at the left eardrum for sound arriving from different directions. Sound arriving from the front is taken as the reference. These curves are the average of measurements on 100 subjects, taken in five countries, over a 40-year period (after Shaw and Vaillancourt).

The total sound pressure acting on the eardrum diaphragm is what actuates the inner workings of the ear. This pressure is affected by the length of the auditory canal, the shape of the head, and the complex of reflections from the pinna interacting with the sound directly entering the canal. This sound pressure not only conveys information on the nature of the source of the sound but also the direction from which it comes. In Fig. 4, the sound arriving directly from the front of the observer is the reference, a fixed sound pressure at all audible frequencies. Sound arriving at the left ear from the left, behind, or the right is markedly different. The ear/brain mechanism interprets these differences to give us directional information.

The outer ear is a far more complex system than a tube with a horn on the end of it. Many early books on hearing considered the pinna a vestigial remnant, useful only for collecting sound. However, modern research is revealing the complex acoustical wonders performed by the pinna and the auditory canal.

The Function of the Middle Ear

The middle ear largely serves a mechanic function, but it's a vital one. It transforms sound energy in air to sound energy in the fluid of the cochlea with maximum efficiency. The sound must reach the oval window of the cochlea. If airborne sound were to impinge directly on the oval window, 99.9 percent of the sound energy would be reflected and only 0.1 percent would get into the cochlea. The reason for this is that air is very tenuous and compressible, while the fluid of the cochlea is dense

and relatively incompressible. The relation between sound pressure and particle velocity in a medium is expressed as the impedance of that medium. Maximum sound energy is transferred from one medium to another when impedances of the two media are matched. The function of the middle ear is to match the impedance of air to that of the fluid of the inner ear. The impedance of the fluid of the cochlea is about 3750 times that of air. The pressure or force ratio required to match the two impedances is the square root of 3750 or 61.

Let us concentrate on those aspects of the middle ear that affect the pressure or force ratio. First, the area of the eardrum is about 80 square millimeters, a ratio of about 27 square millimeters (as shown in Fig. 5A). This means that a certain force acting over the larger eardrum area is concentrated on the smaller oval window area, increasing the pressure on the oval window.

The lever action of the three ossicular bones accounts for an advantage of about 1.32. As shown in Fig. 5B, there is also a certain buckling effect that takes place on the conical eardrum and affects the movement of the attached malleus. This accounts for another factor of 2. The final impedance matching effect is then obtained by multiplying all the individual effects together: $27 \times 1.32 \times 2 = 71$. These very rough estimates account for an overall force ratio of about 71. The disagreement with the 61 calculated from impedance ratios probably reflects our limited knowledge of the factors involved. The agreement is close enough to assure us that the

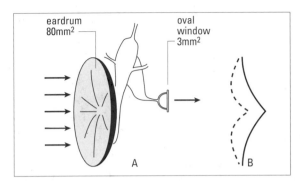

Figure 5 Illustrations of how the sound energy in the tenuous air medium is transferred efficiently to the fluid of the inner ear through the impedance matching function of the middle ear. (A) The force acting on the 80-square-mm area of the eardrum transferred to the 3-square-mm area of the oval window of the inner ear represents a force advantage of 80/3=27. The lever-arm advantage of the ossicles is about 1.32 mm^2. (B) As the conical ear-drum is actuated, a buckling affects the malleus attached to it for an additional factor of two. These factors combine to increase the force on the oval window, conducting the sound to the cochlear fluid with high efficiency.

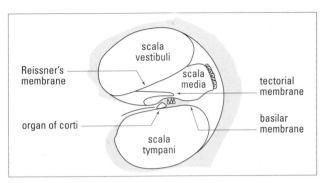

Figure 6 A cross-section of the human cochlea showing the *scala vestibula* and the *scala tympani* with the complex cochlear partition between them. The hair cells in the organ of Corti translate vibrations of the basilar membrane into neural impulses that are sent to the brain via the auditory nerve.

considered factors are the major ones contributing to the middle ear's high efficiency in conducting sound energy from the eardrum to the oval window.

In summary, the ratio of areas between the eardrum and the oval window, the lever action of the ossicles, and the buckling action of the eardrum provide the necessary impedance matching for efficient sound transfer from air to the fluid of the cochlea. Does the system work? Well, an eardrum movement one-tenth the diameter of a hydrogen molecule will produce a perceptible response!

Attached to the ossicles are tiny muscles that tend to limit their movement when very high sound levels actuate the ear. This probably serves to protect the delicate structures of the cochlea. It is especially effective at low frequencies but is too slow to protect against impulsive sounds such as gun shots or hammer blows. It has been demonstrated that this muscular reflex is activated just before one speaks, suggesting that the loudness of one's own speech is reduced. The musculature of the ossicles is also suspected of reducing the masking of higher frequencies by lower frequencies.

The Function of the Inner Ear

Sound waves entering the auditory canal are acoustical in nature. The actuation of the eardrum by this airborne wave sets the ossicles in motion, which in turn, move the oval window of the cochlea. The sound is now in mechanical form. As the oval window moves, it pushes against the fluid of the inner ear. Because this fluid is essentially incompressible, something has to give if the oval window is to move at all. This "give" takes place at the round window (see Fig. 7). When the oval window moves inward, the round window moves outward. As we shall see, this sets up orderly disturbances in the fluid, which through the hair cells, are translated to electrical currents and transmitted to the brain through neural impulses. The sound energy falling on the outer ear goes through the following stages: acoustical, mechanical, electrical, neural. In this section, we will look into what happens in the cochlea, or the inner ear.

In man, the cochlea is embedded deep within solid temporal bone. It is spiral shaped, but for our analytical purposes it is expedient to unroll the spiral to its full 32 millimeter length, or about 1¼ inches. A simplified cross section of the cochlea is shown in Fig. 6. Reissner's membrane defines the chamber known as the *scala vestibuli*. The basilar membrane defines another chamber known as the *scala tympani*. Between these two major chambers is the organ of Corti which contains the hair cells responsible for the actual transduction of the mechanical movement of the membranes to electrical signals. A simplified but useful view of

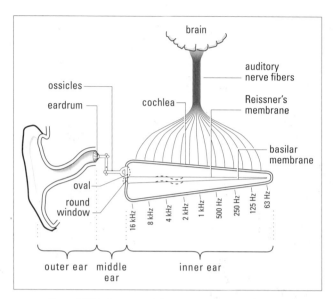

Figure 7 This diagram explains the relationship between the outer, middle, and inner sections of the human ear. The inner ear analyzes the sound. A simple sine wave exciting the ear results in a standing wave effect, causing the basilar membrane to exhibit a peak vibration at a certain place on the membrane. A complex wave would result in a peak for the fundamental and each harmonic.

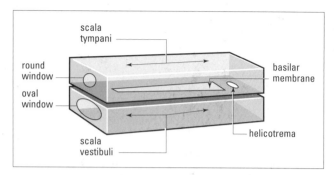

Figure 8 A model of the cochlea made of plastic and filled with a glycerin/water mixture to give the proper viscosity. When sound is introduced into the fluid through the oval window, vibratory peaks on the latex basilar membrane appear that can be studied Such models have been used for many years to study cochlea reaction (after Tonndorf).

the cochlea is to imagine the two *scala* separated by what is known as the *cochlear partition*.

It is with some hesitation that Fig. 7 is presented, but it may help fix in our minds just what takes place in the inner ear. The ossicles are replaced by an oversimplified lever arm, suggesting their function. As the stapes force the liquid inward, the round window bulges out into the middle ear space. The membranes constituting the cochlear partition separate the two chambers for the entire length of the cochlea, except for an opening (called the *helicotrema*) at the apex. Sound entering the cochlear fluid at the oval window sets up traveling waves on the cochlear partition. These traveling waves create localized peak intensities along the cochlear partition, the location of the peak being determined by the frequency of the sound. A complex wave would create numerous peaks with the fundamental and harmonic frequencies. High-frequency peaks occur near the oval and round windows, low-frequency peaks near the apex. In this over-simplified way, we see how the cochlea can be considered an analyzer of sound.

Sensitive hair cells, distributed throughout the length of the cochlear partition, respond to the vibratory peaks set up on the membranes. These hair cells are extensions of the nerve fibers of the auditory nerve.

At this point, we should consider the action of the membranes of the cochlear partition. It has been found that the movement of the basilar membrane dominates, hence our concentration on it. Models have been used extensively in the effort to understand the working of the cochlea. Fig. 8 portrays one of the early models. The case of the model is transparent plastic. The fluid used to simulate the cochlear fluid is a glycerin/water mixture carefully controlled for viscosity. Sandwiched between the two *scala* is the cochlear partition, a thin metal plate that gives support to the latex basilar membrane. When sound is injected through the membrane of the oval window, the peaks of vibration set up on the basilar membrane may be studied.

An important aspect of such model study (as it is with studies centered on actual cochleas) is determining the shape of the vibratory peaks set up by the traveling waves. The sharpness of these peaks influences the preciseness of the analysis of the frequency's dimension. A sharp peak excites fewer hair cells along the organ of Corti than would a broader peak.

Unit 3 demonstrates that it is possible to distinguish between a tone of 1000 Hz and one of 1003 Hz. This is a difference of 0.3 percent and calls for an extremely narrow peak response with very steep sides. The shape of the peaks observed

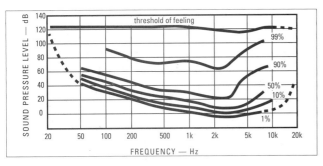

Figure 9 A survey of hearing acuity of a group of typical Americans made by the U.S. Public Health Service. These curves show the least sound that can be heard in dB above the reference level. The 10-percent curve means that 10 percent of the group could hear a sound as weak as or weaker than what the curve indicates.

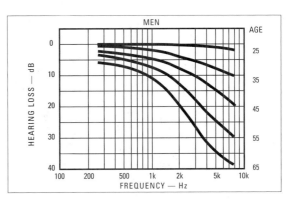

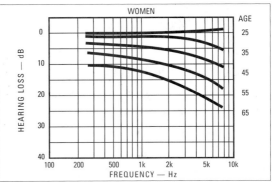

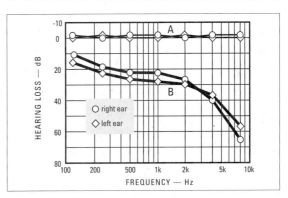

Top to bottom:
Figure 10 Age-related hearing loss in men as a function of age and frequency
Figure 11 Age-related hearing loss in women as a function of age and frequency
Figure 12 Typical audiograms. (A) Audiogram for a person with perfect hearing. (B) Audiogram for a person with a serious hearing impairment. It is generally regarded that an average hearing loss for 500, 1000, and 2000 Hz of 25 dB indicates a hearing handicap.

on the basilar membrane appears far too wide to account for such discriminatory performance by the ear. Inserting microelectrodes into single nerve fibers and counting neural pulses as the frequency changes has revealed very sharp "tuning curves." Recent work on the basilar membrane has revealed ever sharper peaks as experimental methods are improved. This is an active field of study, and the full picture of how the ear achieves its fine analysis is not yet fully known.

Protect Your Hearing!

Our sense of hearing is irreplaceable. All the work being done on cochlear implants offers nothing that approaches the performance of our natural hearing. Therefore, the hearing we now have is all that there is. We may augment deficient hearing with hearing aids, but no hearing aid works as well as our original, undamaged equipment.

The acuity of hearing of a typical group of Americans is shown in Fig. 9. The 1-percent curve represents "normal hearing" for a healthy young adult. Only 1-percent of the population can claim acuity this keen. The 10-percent curve means that 10 percent of the group could hear a sound as weak or weaker than the curve indicates. There is not much room between the 1 percent and 50-percent curves, indicating that half of the population has hearing acuity indicated by the 50-percent curve or the ones below it. Only 1-percent of the group have hearing acuity as bad as the 99-percent curve. The

higher the curve, the louder sounds must be to be heard by the percentage of people indicated. This curve shows that a very significant portion of the population lives with some hearing impairment.

The modern world seems bent on destroying this beautifully contrived hearing system. "Recreational deafness" is a term solidly embedded in today's scientific terminology. Professional sound

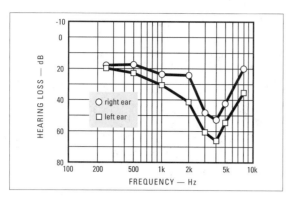

Figure 13 Typical audiogram of person with nerve damage inflicted by excessive noise over a prolonged period of time

mixers working at 110 dB levels are flirting with damaged ears. Some motorcycles and other off-road vehicles can generate hazardous noise levels. Those around firearms are subjected to impulsive noises that sneak through the limiting devices of the middle ear to reach the inner ear unattenuated. The very popular portable music players used with earphones can subject ears to hazardous levels.

What is the effect of the noisy environment? The measurement of many people has given us the information in Fig. 10. In these curves the average hearing loss for men is given as a function of age and frequency. This loss is primarily in the high frequencies and amounts to 20 dB at 8 kHz for a 45-year-old man. Such a high frequency loss means that, for this person, the high partials and overtones of music are attenuated and the musical balance is upset. Timbre, growth, decay, volume, and presence are musical factors most affected by such a loss. Pitch duration, time, vibrato, rhythm, and to some extent, loudness are least affected. The only mistake one has to make to inherit such high-frequency hearing loss is to grow older.

Fig. 11 shows the comparable situation for women. The losses for women are less than those for men. A 45-year-old woman, on the average, will have a loss at 8 kHz of about 11 dB, 9 dB less than a man of the same age.

Self-delusion appears to be a favorite pastime of humans. It seems that those most dependent upon keen and accurate hearing for their livelihood are the most reluctant to admit the possibility of having a hearing impairment. For them to go to an otologist or audiologist for a hearing check-up would be a tacit admission that something is wrong. This is a most unfortunate attitude. Audiograms reveal the truth: either everything is satisfactory or there are problems that should be faced—and the sooner the better. There is no escape from age-related hearing losses. Every informed person knows, or should know, that the older the person, the more the high frequencies drop. The wise musician, audio engineer, or recording mixer will do well to have periodic appraisals of hearing acuity.

Two typical audiograms are shown in Fig. 12. Person A certainly has nothing to fear. Both the right and the left ear exhibit perfect acuity. Person B is at the ragged edge of a serious hearing problem. It is generally considered that an average hearing loss of 25 dB for 500, 1000, and 2000 Hz will be a handicap.

The audiogram of Fig. 13 is a fictitious one, but the big dip in the 3000 to 5000 Hz region is the sort of impairment that results from exposure to excessive sound levels over extended periods of time. It is interesting to note that workers in jute mills at the turn of the century showed the same type of dip that characterizes impairments among modern music workers.

When hearing acuity is reduced, the musician or audio worker turns up the volume to compensate for the loss. This in turn increases the dosage, bringing further damage to the hearing system. A vicious cycle is thus initiated, hastening the deterioration of hearing.

Considerable attention in the units of this course is given to the all-important critical bands. The precision of the analysis of sound taking place in the ear depends upon the sharpness of these critical-band turning curves. It is now recognized that another result of damage to the hair cells is a broadening of the critical bands, which results in coarser frequency analysis and poorer signal-to-noise ratios.

Use of Loudspeakers and Headphones

Some of the experiments and demonstrations in this series require the use of headphones. For example, the masking experiments of Unit 2 definitely require headphones, as does the exploration of binaural beats in Unit 4. To appreciate the experiments of Unit 7, showing how the convolutions of the outer ear give directional cues, headphones are necessary. The true binaural recordings made with the dummy head in Unit 8 can only be fully appreciated by using headphones. Headphones of good quality should be used. Here is a tabulation of the points in the series requiring headphones:

Unit	Loudspeakers	Headphones
1. Loudness, Pitch, and Timbre	All	
2. How One Sound Masks Another		All
3. How the Ear Analyzes Sound	All	
4. Non-Linearities in the Auditory System	Beginning and end	Central portion
5. The Perception of Delayed Sounds	All	
6. Why Some Sounds Are More Pleasant Than Others	All	
7. How We Locate Sounds	First part	Last part
8. True Binaural Listening		All

Loudness, Pitch, and Timbre

The subjective correlates of sound level, frequency, and spectrum

Talk

Tech

An audio engineer has available an impressive array of instruments for measuring the physical aspects of sound.

One is the sound level meter, by which he can readily measure sound pressure level or intensity as it is also known.

Another is the electronic counter, which can faithfully count each cycle of a periodic sound wave and thus determine its frequency.

He also has a spectrum analyzer that reveals at a glance the harmonic structure of a complex periodic wave.

These instruments and others all operate in the realm of applied physics. They measure only the physical attributes of the sound as it comes to our ears.

The response of our ears to that sound stimulus exists in an entirely different realm: the realm of psychoacoustics.

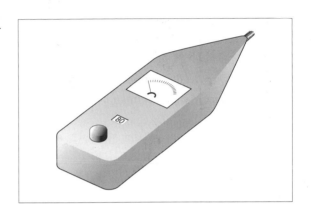

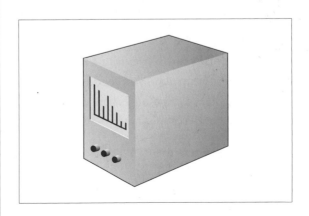

Talk

Tech

There are no subjective instruments or meters that can give us direct readings of the response of an individual to different physical stimuli. Each person responds in a different way. The only way to measure human response to different sounds is by psychoacoustic testing. Panels of observers or listeners are the very heart of such experiments, and their response must be statistically analyzed to get dependable answers.

No longer can audio people take the ear for granted. The auditory response to speech and music vibrations in the air must be taken into careful consideration, for human perception is the final link in the audio chain.

Let's first explore the relationship between the physical aspect of a sound, its sound pressure level, and loudness, the ears' subjective response to it.

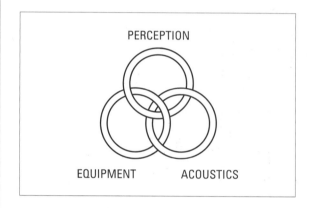

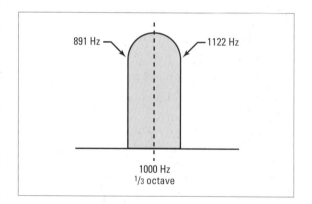

One of our first discoveries is that our ears are more sensitive to mid-band sounds than low-frequency sounds. For example, here is a one-third octave band of noise centered on 1000 Hz:

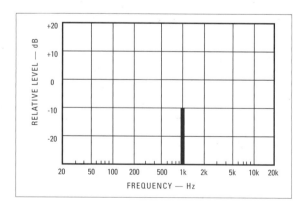

Now we will hear a one-third octave band of noise at the same level centered on 50 Hz:

The 50-Hz noise sounds softer to us because our ears are so insensitive to 50 Hz that we barely hear the noise at all.

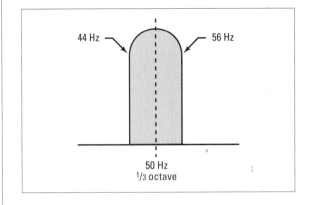

In order to be able to hear the low-frequency band of noise at subjectively the same loudness, it must be more intense. Here is the same one-third octave band of noise centered on 50 Hz at a sound pressure level about 20 dB higher than the 1000 Hz noise:

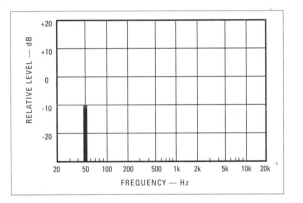

It takes about a 20 dB increase in level for the low-frequency noise to have the same apparent loudness as the noise at 1000 Hz.

The decreased sensitivity of our ears at both low and high frequencies is very noticeable when we listen to music at low levels.

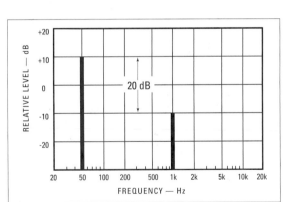

A typical musical selection sounds like this at normal listening level:

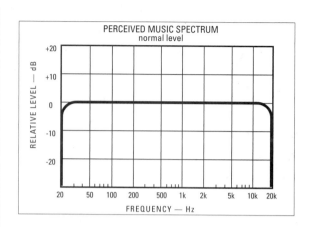

The same musical passage played at a level 20 dB lower sounds deficient in lows and highs:

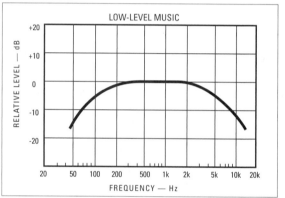

Playback at such low levels requires boosting lows and highs to restore a semblance of quality:

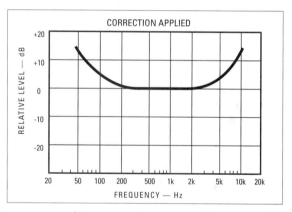

This is the principle of the so-called *loudness equalization*, which is practiced by high-fidelity enthusiasts.

The equalization required to make low-level music sound right comes close to tracing an equal-loudness contour. However, equal-loudness contours are actually found by testing hundreds of subjects. Each contour is referred to a sound-pressure level at 1000 Hz.

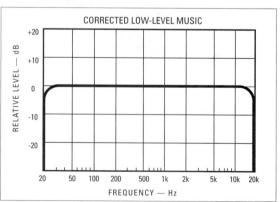

Talk

Tech

Let's say we set the sound pressure level at a subject's ears to 40 dB at 1000 Hz. Changing the frequency of the signal to 500 Hz, the subject is asked to adjust the level until it sounds as loud as the 1000-Hz signal. This process is repeated for many other frequencies throughout the audible band until that contour is completely defined. Many other listeners also compare the loudness of tones of other frequencies to that of the 1000-Hz tone. The average of the responses delineate an equal-loudness contour that goes through the 40-dB point at 1000 Hz.

By a similar process, other contours are traced, each tied down to a specific sound-pressure level at 1000 Hz. These levels at 1000 Hz are arbitrarily called *loudness levels* in phons.

This loudness level is a physical measurement and must not be equated to subjective loudness. However, the same subjective loudness (of unknown value) does prevail along each contour, and for this reason, these contours have many practical applications.

The family of equal-loudness contours reveals much about the average ear's comparative response in terms of loudness. The lowest contour is the threshold of hearing, the average minimum audible sound.

The 120-phon contour is close to the threshold of pain and ear damage. The 120-dB loudness range means that the ear can handle sound levels ranging from the sound of air molecules bouncing off the eardrum up to the sound of a nearby rocket blastoff or excessively loud amplified music.

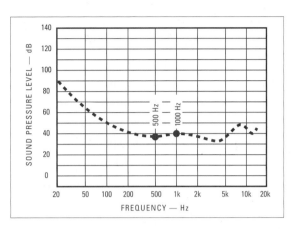

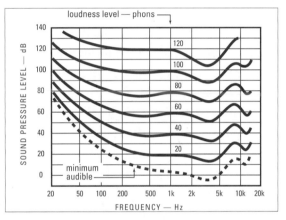

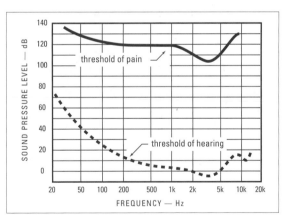

In other words, the power of the loudest sound is a million, million times that of the softest sound the ear can handle.

Another interesting aspect of equal-loudness contours is that the minimum-audible curve is really an average audiogram of the hundreds of subjects participating in the experiment.

When you go to an otologist or a clinical audiologist to have your hearing tested, your audiogram is really your own personal minimum audible equal-loudness contour!

Equal-loudness contours are of interest to audio people in that they tell something about the frequency response of the ear. By inverting the 30-phon contour, the frequency response of that loudness level is obtained. Similarly, by inverting the 90-phon contour, the frequency response at the 90-phon loudness level results.

This shows that the frequency response of our auditory system changes with the sound level.

We have barely scratched the surface in treating the loudness characteristics of human hearing. Our principle emphasis here is that subjective loudness and physical-sound-level meter readings can only be correlated through psychoacoustical measurement techniques involving human listeners.

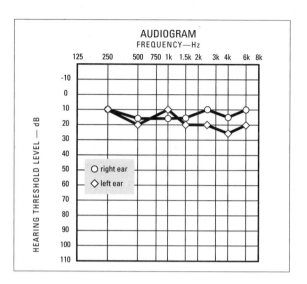

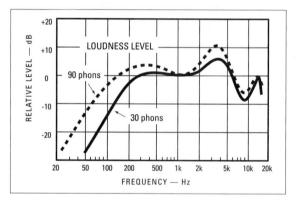

One way to define pitch is that attribute of sound which, when varied, can result in melody.

Pitch is another strictly subjective concept.

Pitch is related to the repetition rate of the waveform of sound. For a pure tone, pitch is related to frequency. The following pure tone has a specific and definite pitch:

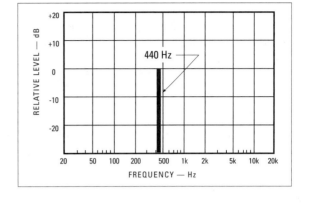

This tone corresponds in frequency to the standard A 440 note on the piano:

There is a curious phenomenon called *low pitch* in which complex tones tend to have a slightly lower subjective pitch than pure tones of the same frequency.

In the following comparison, the A note on the piano and the pure tone from the oscillator have been carefully adjusted with an electronic counter to have exactly the same frequency:

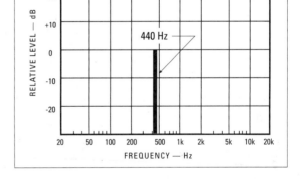

Does the pitch of the piano note seem to be slightly lower than that of the pure tone? The presence of the partials in the complex tone has to be responsible for this effect, because the fundamentals of both are pure tones of identical frequency.

Low pitch is an interesting, but minor, effect. In general, the pitch of a complex tone is that frequency associated with its fundamental. The harmonics have only a minor effect on the perceived pitch of a complex tone.

Pitch is generally considered as a one-dimensional effect, running continuously from low to high. For example, we can play the 12 tones of the chromatic scale and move from middle C to the C above:

This illustrates that pitch has the dimension of what might be called height. Traveling from middle C to the C above in this way, however, is by semitone increments. But the continuous nature of pitch height may be illustrated by sweeping pink noise with a one-third octave filter:

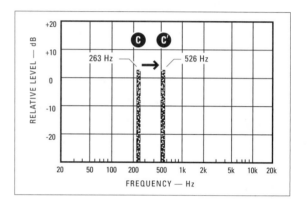

In the case of tones richly endowed with harmonics, pitch becomes a much more complicated matter. By carefully controlling the amplitude and frequencies of the components of harmonically rich tones, it is possible to move from one tone to another along different paths.

It is possible to move progressively in tone, for example, from middle C up one octave and find oneself right back at the starting point! This is called *circularity of pitch.*

The following is a demonstration of circular pitch created by computer manipulations of the amplitudes and frequencies of the various tones:

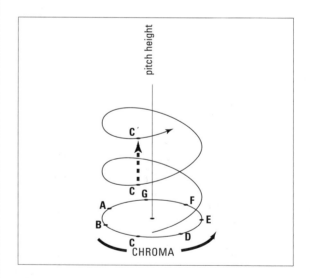

Each upward step in pitch height is compensated for by an increase in the amplitude of the low-frequency components and slight decrease in amplitude of the high-frequency components. The idea of pitch having dimensions other than height is becoming well established.

Even though the harmonics of a complex tone have little effect on the pitch of that tone, harmonics are the very essence of the timbre, or tonal quality, of musical or other sounds.

Let us start with the simplest tone possible: a pure sine wave having a frequency of 1000 Hz:

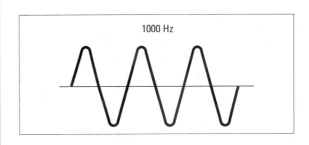

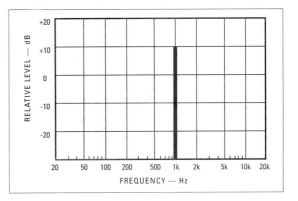

The timbre of a pure tone is rather thin and emaciated to say the least.

If we distort this sine wave by clipping the positive and negative peaks, harmonics are generated and the quality, or timbre, of the sound is changed:

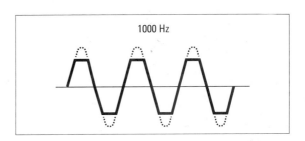

The clipped sine wave has a different quality, or timbre, than that of the pure tone:

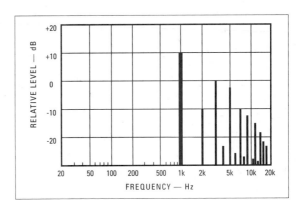

If the clipping process is carried to its extreme, a square wave results. Because the square wave has yet a different harmonic structure, its timbre is different from that of the clipped sine wave:

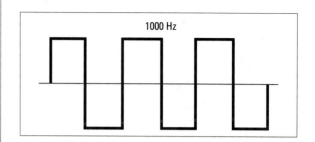

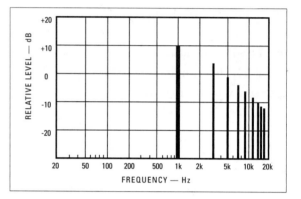

And so it is with musical notes:

We have no trouble identifying these instruments from a small sample of their sound.

The fundamental frequency of each instrument was the standard A or 440 cycles per second. The difference lies entirely in the unique train of harmonics or partials of each.

The sound of each instrument's tone has essentially the same loudness and the same pitch, but they differ greatly in timbre. In addition to harmonics, certain temporal effects such as rise time, vibrato, etc. must also be included in the concept of timbre.

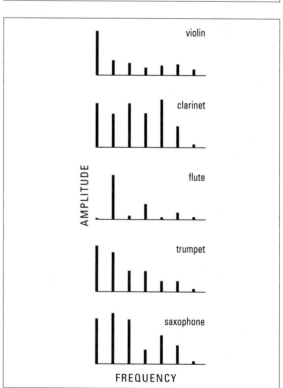

The "case of the missing fundamental" casts an interesting sidelight on timbre. Let's consider three pure tones: 400, 600, and 1000 Hz:

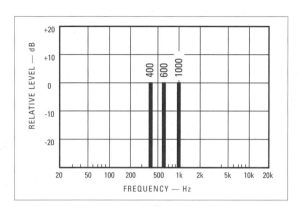

There are three distinct pitches, since each tone has its own pitch.

Now, let's see what happens when all three are sounded together:

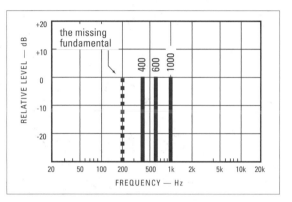

The pitch of the combination is not that of the 400-, the 600-, or even the 1000-Hz tone; neither is it a mixture or average of the three.

Rather, what we hear is the pitch of a 200-Hz tone!:

Now, what is so significant about a 200-Hz frequency? Let's look closely at this.

One clue is that 400 and 600 are 200 Hz apart. Also, 600 and 1000 are twice 200 Hz apart.

Everything comes together and is understandable if these three tones are considered as harmonics of a 200-Hz fundamental. Thus, the pitch of the combination turns out to be that associated with a 200-Hz fundamental which isn't there at all!

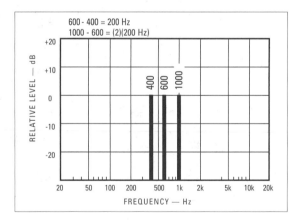

The ear/brain auditory system has it all figured out that only a fundamental of 200 Hz makes sense of these three tones considered as harmonics.

In summary, we have considered certain aspects of loudness, pitch, and timbre which are subjective characteristics of sound. There are no instruments for direct measurement of these dimensions of sound. The responses of many people in a psychoacoustic type of test are the only way to quantify these factors.

Sound-pressure level is a physical correlate for loudness, but the two terms may not be equated. In a similar way, frequency is a physical correlate for pitch, and spectrum is a physical correlate for timbre. But it is imperative that we do not confuse the physical stimulus with the psychoacoustical response.

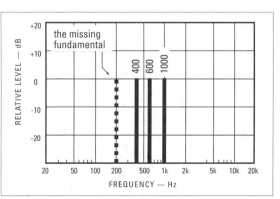

How One Sound Masks Another
A study of critical bands

  Talk   Tech

In this section, we recommend that you listen with headphones rather than loudspeakers.

 (Distant male voice) "Ah...Dixie, what time is Andre getting home tonight?"

 (Close female voice) "What? You know I can't hear you when the water's running!"

 Now that was a perfect example of the masking of one sound by another. The sound of running water masks, or obscures, the voice. Other examples of masking are constantly around us:

 In an automobile, the noise of the engine, tires, and whistling wind tends to mask the sound of the radio, and we have to turn up the volume.

 In open-area offices, privacy is often a problem:

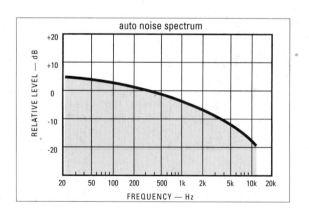

Talk · Tech

It may be desirable to keep conversations like this from being understood in the next cubicle. This can be done by what is euphemistically called *acoustical perfume*. Loudspeakers throughout the open office area radiate a sound like this:

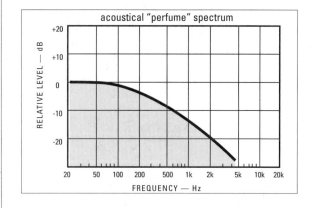

Some people think this sound is soothing, like the sound of water running in a brook. Others say it is just one more noise in an already noisy world!

Whatever your view, the noise is capable of masking low-level voices:

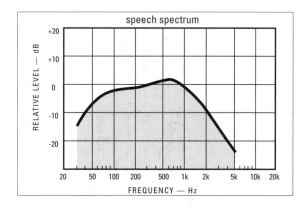

Knowing how the human hearing system responds to masking noises can be valuable and practical.

Psychologists first studied how one tone like this:

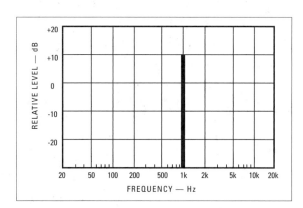

Can be masked by another tone like this:

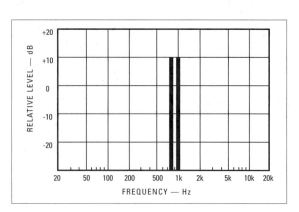

If you were to listen to this recording over loudspeakers instead of headphones, standing waves in the room would be troublesome. The loudness of a tone would then be effected by the position of your head, and this would tend at times to obscure the point of the demonstration. Do not be afraid to move your head to hear a sound better. You might wish to stop and repeat the following section of the recording, listening both ways for comparison.

Here is a 1000-Hz tone at a low but clearly audible level:

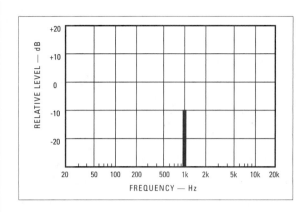

Next, we will introduce a second tone, an 800-Hz tone, at about the same level:

Both tones are now clearly audible.

Now let's see how much of the 800-Hz tone it will take to mask the 1000-Hz tone. Here are the two tones again, at equal levels:

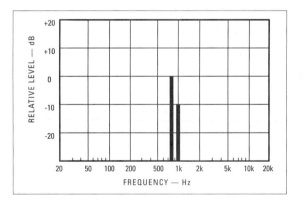

Now we'll increase the level of the 800-Hz tone by 10 dB:

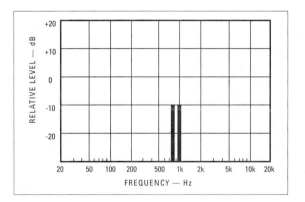

The 1000-Hz tone is still audible, so we'll boost the 800-Hz tone another 5 dB:

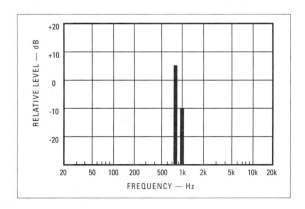

Talk   Tech

The 1000-Hz tone is still audible, so we increase the 800-Hz masking tone another 5 dB:

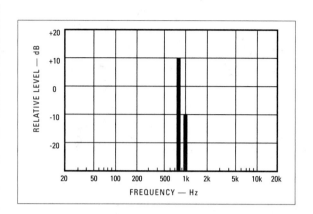

At this point, you may want to listen to this recording the other way. Some people will still hear the 1000-Hz tone and some may not. We will not carry this experiment any further, lest these monotonous sounds drive you crazy! Furthermore, the actual level of masking varies somewhat with the individual. That is why panels of listeners are used in psychoacoustical testing. The point we are making is that the 800-Hz tone can drown out the 1000-Hz tone if its level is increased sufficiently.

Now, be sure your headphones are back on.

Psychologists got into trouble with pure tone masking experiments. When the masking tone is very close to the frequency of the tone being masked, the most interesting region, interference beats occur, making meaningful measurements impossible:

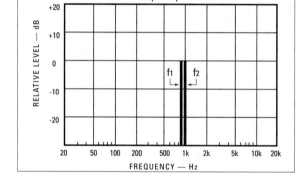

These beats create serious problems for experimenters utilizing pure tones in masking tests.

In 1940, Harvey Fletcher, a scientist at Bell Laboratories, studied the masking of tones by using broad-band random noise, called *white noise*. The sound energy of a tone is concentrated at its specific frequency, but the energy of white noise is distributed uniformly throughout the entire audible spectrum. White noise sounds like this:

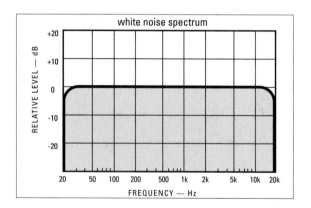

Fletcher ran a series of experiments with trained observers to determine how effectively this noise can mask tones of different frequencies. We'll repeat one such experiment now. Let's try to mask our 1000-Hz tone by broad-band noise. Here again is our 1000-Hz tone:

Now we'll introduce the masking noise at an equal overall level:

Notice that the tone is still quite audible. Now, the level of the noise will be increased in 5-dB steps until we reach a point at which the tone becomes inaudible (to the average listener, at least):

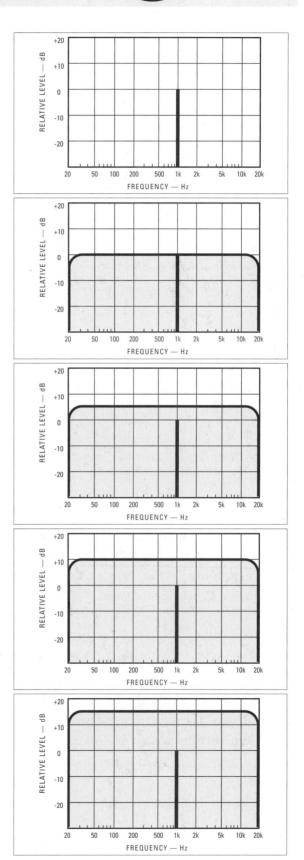

Talk

Tech

We have had to increase the noise level 20 dB above the level of the tone in order to mask it effectively.

Fletcher came to the conclusion that only that noise energy which is very close to the tone in frequency was effective in masking the tone.

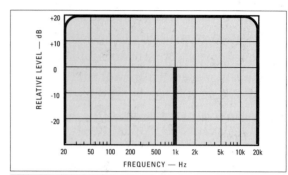

Let's see if this is true.

Let's see how effective the noise is in masking the 1000-Hz tone if we chop off the noise energy below 200 Hz and above 5000 Hz:

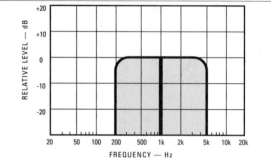

We still have to increase the level of the noise by 20 dB to mask the tone.

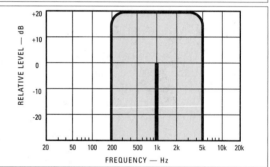

Now let's reduce the noise band even more. This time we eliminate the noise energy below 500 Hz and above 2500 Hz. Now we'll see how effective it is in masking the tone:

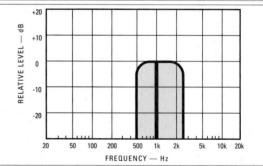

We still have to increase the noise 20 dB to mask the tone. The noise energy we have eliminated seems to have no effect on masking the tone.

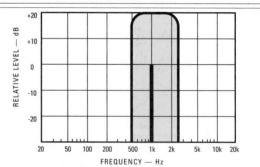

Well, that is exactly what Fletcher said. Only the noise energy close to the frequency of the tone is effective in masking the tone.

The band of noise from 500 Hz to 2500 Hz is 2000 Hz wide. Fletcher continued to reduce the width of the noise band until it finally affected the masking of the tone. When the noise band was narrower than about 100 Hz, the masking of the 1000-Hz tone was definitely affected.

Fletcher repeated this experiment at many frequencies. The bandwidth of the noise just beginning to affect the masking of a particular tone he called *the critical band*, effective at that frequency.

Fletcher's work encouraged other scientists to explore the shape of these so-called critical bands of the human hearing system. Instead of using two tones, which produced beats, some experimenters used one tone and a band of noise much narrower than the critical band, such as this:

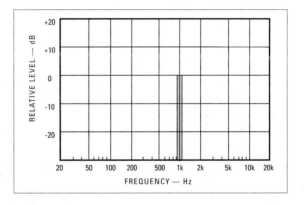

This band of noise is one-tenth of an octave wide and is centered on 1000 Hz. Actually, it extends from 966 Hz to 1035 Hz and sounds much like a fluctuating tone of about 1000 Hz.

Now, let's try masking this one-tenth octave band of noise by tones of different frequencies.

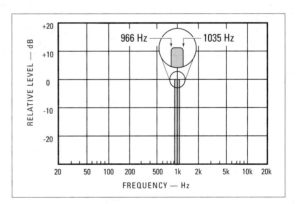

Talk   Tech

This is a 700-Hz tone:

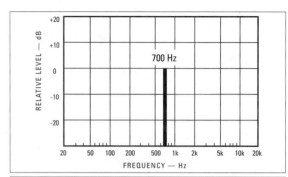

Now, let's listen to the noise and the tone together to get used to them:

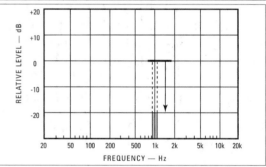

To keep our masking experiment within the available dynamic range of this recording, we must reduce the noise to a lower level:

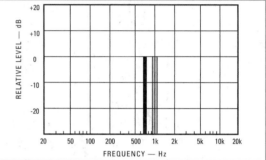

Now, as we listen intently to the noise signal, the level of the 700-Hz tone will be increased:

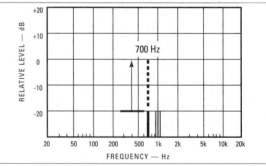

The level of the 700-Hz tone is now 20 dB higher than that of the noise band centered on 1000 Hz, but the noise is still audible.

Let's increase the level of the 700-Hz tone still further:

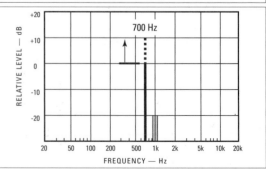

Now, for most people, the noise is completely masked, but some will still hear it because each person's hearing is unique. But we can all agree that to mask the noise, the 700-Hz tone must be *about* 30 dB higher than the one-tenth octave band of noise centered on 1000 Hz.

This is one point on our masking curve: approximately 30 dB at 700 Hz.

To find another point on the curve, we turn our attention to 800 Hz. By increasing its level, the point at which it masks the 1000-Hz noise is found to be somewhere around 25 dB:

The level of the 900-Hz tone must be increased only about 18 dB to mask the noise:

We now have three points on our masking curve.

Tones of 700, 800, and 900 Hz are all of lower frequency than the 1000-Hz noise band. Now, let's try tones above 1000 Hz. First, 1100 Hz:

Like 900 Hz, we find that the 1100-Hz tone must be increased about 18 dB to mask the noise band centered on 1000 Hz. This is another point on our masking curve.

Now for 1200 Hz:

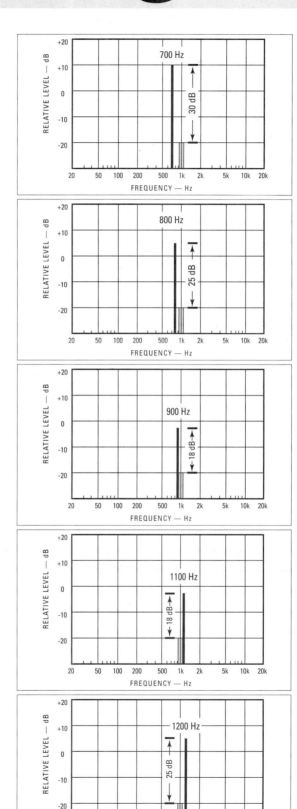

While this experiment is far from exact, we find that the 1200-Hz tone must be increased about 25 dB to mask the noise.

Finally, let's try 1300 Hz:

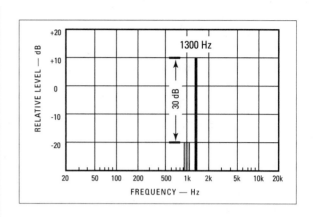

A masking tone 300 Hz above the noise seems to have roughly the same effect as one 300 Hz below the noise centered on 1000 Hz.

Plotting all six points together delineates the masking audiogram of 1000 Hz, or to put it in another way, it shows the shape of the ear's critical band at 1000 Hz.

Simply stated, the closer the *probe tone* is to the noise band, the easier it is to mask the noise. That's exactly what Fletcher said: Only sound energy near a tone of a given frequency is effective in masking it.

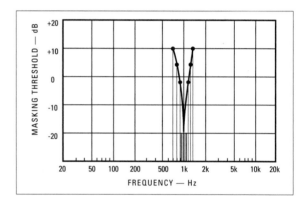

Audio engineers don't generally think in terms of masking audiograms or critical bands; indeed, they think in terms of filters. The critical band we have just discovered is really a filter. If we think in terms of attenuation, we can invert the curve of masking thresholds—which will give us the critical band in traditional filter form.

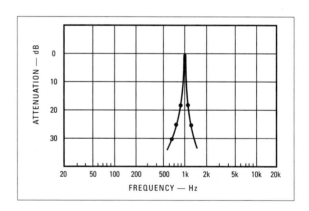

It is interesting to note that the ear's filter bandwidths are not too far from one-third octaves.

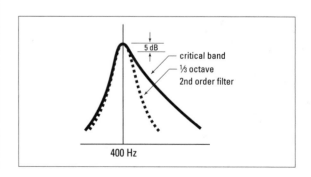

Talk

Tech

The audio engineer will then say, "Aha! The ear is just like our common one-third octave filter sets." But not so. True, there may be some similarity in filter shape, but the similarity ends there.

A one-third octave filter set is made up of adjacent filters that overlap at points 3 dB down, so that some 27 filters cover the entire 20 Hz to 20,000 Hz audible range. The ear's critical band filter set is far more complex and sophisticated.

In this experiment, we have explored in detail sound around a frequency of 1000 Hz. A similarly shaped critical band filter can be found centered at any specific frequency in the audible band.

If we move up or down in frequency just a few hertz, we will find a new critical band awaiting us. Critical bands are not adjacent, like the filters in the one-third octave filter set, but have continuously overlapping center frequencies. There are literally thousands of critical bands in our auditory system.

Any sound that reaches our ears and brain is analyzed by this all-pervasive filtering process.

In coming demonstrations, we will see how important the critical bands are in sensing the timbre of musical sounds and in determining whether musical tones are consonant or dissonant.

Whatever new things are discovered in the future about our perception of sounds, it now seems highly probable that the critical band will play a central role.

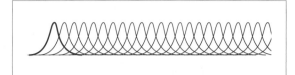

How the Ear Analyzes Sound
Auditory filters at work

In the very act of listening to music, the sound is unconsciously broken down into its component parts by our ear/brain system. But before we can study what the ear does, we must make sure we understand the difference between simple and complex tones.

Sounding the standard A on an electronic oscillator yields what is called a *monotone*:

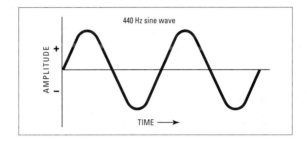

The word *monotonous*, which comes from the words *mono* and *tone*, is a good description of this sound—plain and uninteresting.

Sounding the standard A on a good violin yields a much richer sound:

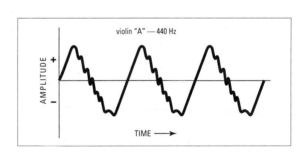

The difference between the pure sine wave of the oscillator and the comparable note of the violin is what music is all about.

The violin has a quality, a timbre, which is pleasing to our ears:

Talk

Tech

The vibration of the violin string itself is a complex process. In fact, it can vibrate at many frequencies at the same time.

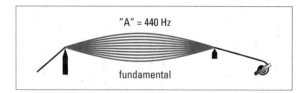

When the tension and length of the string are just right (or *in tune*, as we would say), bowing the string sets it to vibrating at the standard A, which is defined at 440 vibrations per second, or 440 Hz. This number of vibrations per second is called the *fundamental frequency*:

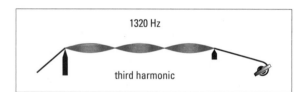

Now, the interesting thing is that this same string, with the same tension and length, also vibrates at twice 440 or 880 Hz. The 440-Hz vibration (the fundamental frequency) is called the first harmonic, and the 880-Hz vibration is called the second harmonic:

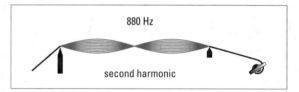

The same bowing action also sets the string to vibrating at three times the fundamental frequency. Three times 440 is 1320 Hz. This is called the third harmonic:

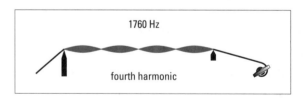

There is also a fourth harmonic at 1760 Hz:

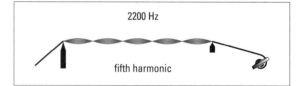

...and a fifth harmonic at 2200 Hz:

...and so on.

Talk

Tech

The fundamental, or first, harmonic, is usually the strongest, and normally the higher the order of the harmonic, the weaker it is.

The harmonic array of the violin tone gives it the richness and specific character which we recognize as coming from the violin. Each instrument in the orchestra has its own particular harmonic signature. The number and relative intensities of these constituent tones determine the quality, or timbre, of that particular instrument.

The wave analyzer is a special electronic instrument that automatically plots the spectrum of any signal applied to its input terminals. For example, the pure 440-Hz tone from the oscillator has no harmonics. All its energy is concentrated at a single frequency:

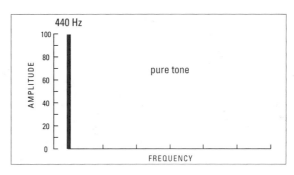

The violin sounding the standard A at 440 Hz, however, has its own characteristic train of harmonics, all of which are multiples of the fundamental:

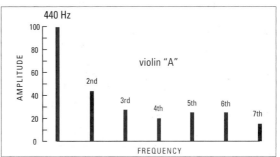

The clarinet sounding an A has the same 440-Hz fundamental followed by its own unique array of harmonics which make it sound like a clarinet:

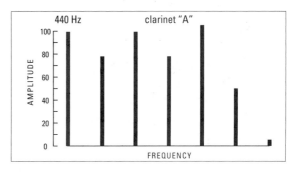

The synthesizer can give us an A with almost any harmonic structure desired. Here are two different synthesizer notes, both having 440-Hz fundamentals:

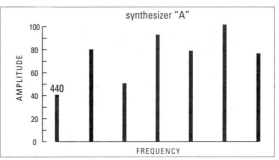

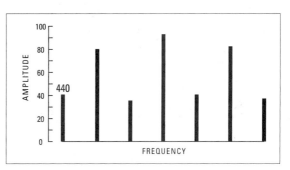

If we can tell the difference between the sound of the clarinet and the sound of the violin sounding the same note, there is only one conclusion: that the human auditory system can function as a wave analyzer! It is capable of sorting out the harmonics of the violin and clarinet sounds and sensing their relative amplitudes.

Let's see what each of us can do in "hearing out" the harmonics of the violin A sound. To refresh our memories, here is the violin sound again:

There is no problem recognizing the fundamental, as this is the pitch of the tone:

The second harmonic is twice the frequency of the 440-Hz fundamental, or 880 Hz:

Now, as the violin sounds its A, concentrate your attention not on the fundamental but on the 880 Hz, and see if you can hear out that second harmonic. To help calibrate your mind's frequency scale, an 880-Hz tone will be injected now and then:

It isn't easy, is it? Don't be discouraged if you have not made contact yet. This is a rather abstract business, but more chances are coming.

The third harmonic of the violin A falls at 1320 Hz:

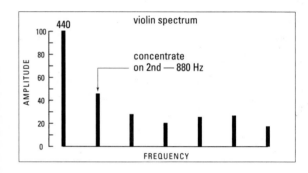

Let's see if we can pick out that third harmonic from the violin tone. As before, a tracer tone of 1320 Hz will be injected briefly at times to help us concentrate on that frequency:

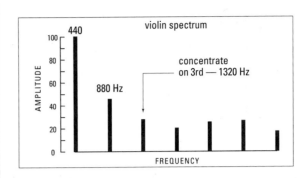

Usually, the higher the harmonic, the weaker it is. In spite of this, let's see what our ears and brains can do on the fifth harmonic of the violin A at 2200 Hz. First, we'll listen to that frequency to see what it sounds like:

Now, concentrate hard for this fifth harmonic:

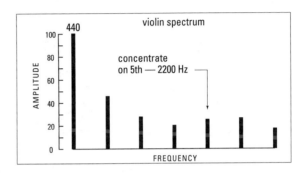

With no cue tones for the next 20 seconds, let the personal wave analyzer in your head range up and down the frequency scale to see how many harmonics you can hear out:

We have or at least we have tried to hear out harmonics of the violin tone up to the fifth harmonic. What is the highest harmonic that can be heard?

Research has shown that a prime requisite of the ability to hear out a harmonic in a complex wave is that the separation between adjacent harmonics must be greater than the critical bandwidth. If two adjacent harmonics fall within a common critical band, the ear cannot distinguish one from the other.

When we consider the seventh and eighth harmonics, we find the critical bandwidth to be about 500 Hz wide. As these harmonics are only separated by 440 Hz, we would expect that the possibility of hearing out the seventh and eighth harmonics would be very small. This is exactly what researchers have found.

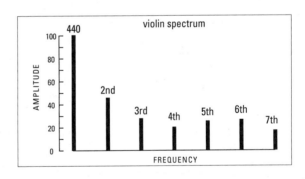

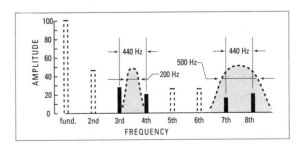

Talk   **Tech**

It seems that every time we study a new facet of our hearing, we find critical bands are required to explain it. All this means that the ear is basically like a Fourier analyzer—to use a term familiar to electronics people. We use this analyzing ability of our auditory system all the time without giving it a thought.

In addition to hearing out the harmonics of a complex tone, the ear has remarkable powers of discrimination.

With the people talking all around us, we can direct our attention to one person, subjectively pushing other conversations into the background. We can direct our attention to one group of instruments in an orchestra or to one singer in a choir. Listening to someone talk in the presence of high background noise, we are able to select out the talk and reject, to a degree, the noise. This is all done subconsciously, but we are constantly using this amazing faculty.

We can also use this ability to discriminate between different tones which are close together in frequency. For example, this is our familiar 1000-Hz tone:

This is a tone only 10 Hz higher:

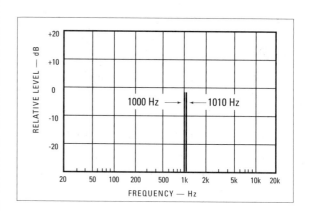

We have no difficulty telling the difference between them when we hear them one after the other:

This is 1 percent discrimination.

Can we distinguish tones only 3 Hz apart? Let's try it:

Most people can tell the difference between the two. This is a discrimination of only three-tenths of 1 percent. All this with common, run of the mill, untrained ears!

How can frequency discrimination of three-tenths of 1 percent be explained? In the first lesson, we were introduced to critical bands. As the widths of critical bands are from 15 to 20 percent of the frequency being considered, at 1000 Hz, the critical band is about 150 Hz wide. How can bands this wide possibly account for frequency discriminations of three-tenths of 1 percent?

Psychologists have suspected some sort of second filter upstream in the ear/brain system. By inserting microelectrodes into single auditory nerve fibers and then measuring the firing rate of nerve impulses, they found extremely narrow tuning curves. Whether these steep-sided tuning curves are sufficient to explain three-tenths of 1 percent frequency discrimination is still being studied. There may be some time processing as well. At any rate, we stand in awe of the precision the auditory system exhibits.

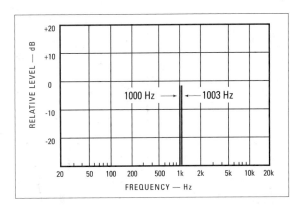

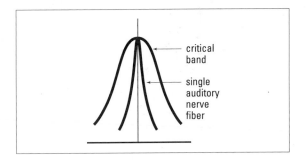

It is also possible to use the analytical ability of our ears to measure the shape of the spectrum of any common noise, such as this one:

Sound familiar? That noise was recorded in an automobile traveling 55 miles per hour on a freeway. The energy in this noise is distributed throughout the audible spectrum in a way unknown to us. But by using the critical bands in our heads, we shall find out how the energy is distributed from low frequencies to high frequencies.

We'll make the car our masking noise, and a pure tone will be our exploring probe. First, we will use this 125-Hz tone:

We will adjust the level of the 125-Hz tone until the car noise energy in the critical band centered on this frequency just masks the tone:

The level of the tone is now -15 dB. The tone is clearly audible in the car noise, so we'll reduce the level of the tone by 5 dB:

The tone can still be heard, but we are closer to the point at which the car noise masks the tone. I shall now reduce the level of the tone until it is just masked by the noise as I hear it:

Now, the level of the tone is about -23 dB. To my ears, this is the masking threshold at 125 Hz. You may or may not agree with me, but we are illustrating a principle rather than trying for precise, universal results. Each set of ears is unique, and differences are to be expected.

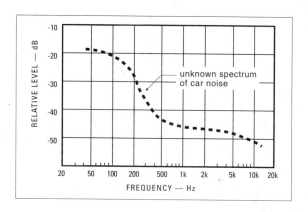

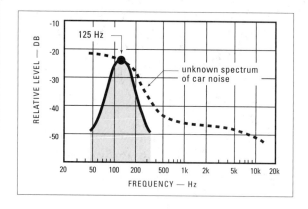

But let's go on to another frequency, 500 Hz:

The 500-Hz tone is clearly audible in the car noise. Now, we'll decrease the level of the tone 5 dB:

The tone is still audible, so let's reduce it until it is just masked by the car noise in the critical band centered on 500 Hz:

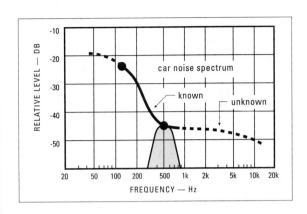

There. To my ears, the tone reaches threshold at a level of -44 dB. That is a second point on our curve.

For a third point on our car noise spectrum curve, let us use a probe tone of 2000 Hz:

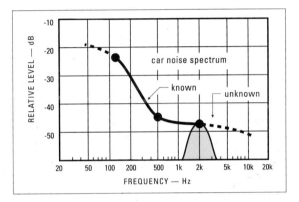

Now, the 2000-Hz probe tone level will be gradually reduced until it is just masked by the car noise:

For me, the level of the 2000-Hz tone is -46 dB at threshold. We now have three points on our car noise spectrum curve. We find that as frequency is increased, the energy level of the car noise tends to fall off. This is typical of many noises in our environment. Now many other points could be plotted to reveal greater detail of the shape of our car noise spectrum.

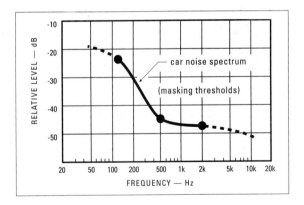

We must call this a *critical band spectrum* because each point is dependent upon the width of the critical band at each measuring frequency. Its shape will be very close to that of a spectrum measured with a one-third octave analyzer because critical bandwidths are not too far from one-third octave bandwidths.

We must pause here to reconsider the significance of what we have just done. We have determined the spectral shape of a common environmental noise by using the critical bands in our auditory system as the analyzer. This is based on the principle that only the noise energy within the critical band centered on the probe tone frequency is effective in masking the tone.

So, what have we done? We have demonstrated the remarkable analytical ability of our hearing system—an ability which we use all the time without giving it a second thought. And that isn't all. Other equally astounding characteristics of the human ear will be demonstrated in future lessons.

Non-Linearities in the Auditory System

Distortions generated in the ear

Talk   **Tech**

Distortion in amplifiers, loudspeakers, and other pieces of audio equipment is a matter of deep concern, not only to the designers of such equipment, but also to those using it. High-fidelity sound requires low distortion in each link of the audio chain, because the distortion of each link adds to that of other links.

All this attention to distortion in equipment is for the purpose of preserving the full quality and naturalness of the original sound through the transmission, recording, and reproduction processes.

A system that is truly linear delivers at its output terminals a perfect replica of the signal applied to its input terminals.

A non-linear system alters the input wave-form and delivers a distorted signal at the output. The distorted output contains frequency components not in the input signal. Non-linearity always means distortion, and distortion always adds to the input signal something new and undesirable that wasn't there before. As with amplifiers and other audio equipment, this is also true of the human auditory system. But before we examine distortion in the ear, let's focus attention on the distortion process itself.

When the signal applied exceeds the limits of the system, the waveform of the signal is distorted and new frequency components or distortion products are generated. This is true of all audio systems, whether physical or physiological.

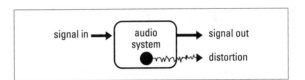

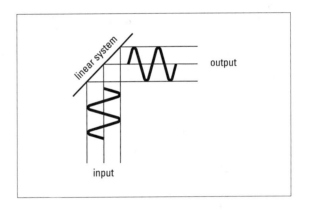

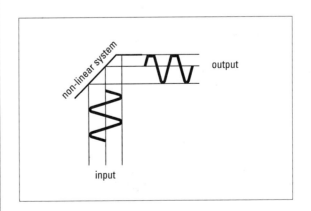

Talk   **Tech**

Let's apply a pure sine wave of 1000 Hz to our distorting system. The spectrum of this input signal shows all energy concentrated at a single frequency:

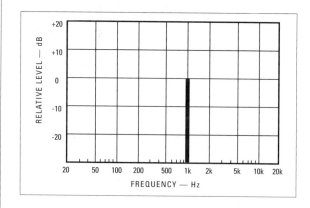

The spectrum of the output signal has harmonics at 2000, 3000, and 4000 Hz, and other multiples of 1000 Hz. We can hear a noticeable difference between the sounds as they are compared:

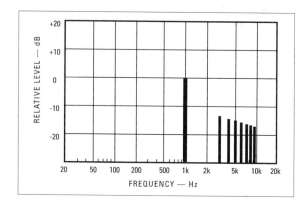

For the balance of this section, you should be wearing headphones in order to achieve proper results from the listening tests. If you're not already doing so, please put them on now.

You are now going to hear a pure 150-Hz sine wave signal at a fairly low level, just to become accustomed to its sound:

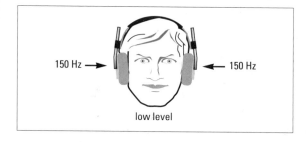

Talk   **Tech**

At this lower level, the harmonics generated in the ear are not very noticeable. In order to hear these aural harmonics, the level must be increased. As you listen to the following 150-Hz signal (played at a higher level), see if you can also detect the weaker harmonics at 300 Hz and other multiples of 150 Hz. If it seems too loud to you, reduce the playback volume somewhat. Be careful not to damage your ears:

Don't be too disappointed if you do not detect them, but they are there all right. It just takes a bit of practice.

Another method for detecting the presence of aural harmonics is by playing the fundamental frequency into the left earphone and injecting a probe tone at the frequency of a harmonic in the right ear and listening for a binaural beat. Now, listening to the same 150-Hz pure tone, we'll do a bit of probing with a tone close to 300 Hz. You will hear a beat as the probe tone comes close to the second harmonic of the 150-Hz fundamental:

These aural harmonics are produced by non-linearities of the ear and do not exist as external signals. Thus, they are inaccessible to any physical measuring instruments. However, their presence can be verified through these binaural beats. In fact, knowing that strongest beats are produced when the two signals are close to the same amplitude, scientists are able not only to detect the presence of aural harmonics but also to estimate their amplitudes.

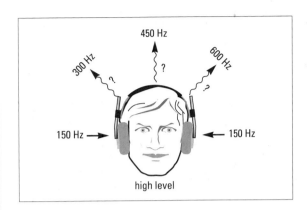

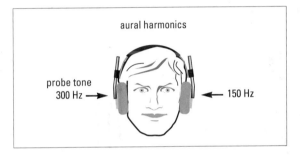

Let's do some probing for other aural harmonics. With the 150-Hz tone producing harmonics every 150 Hz up through the spectrum, let's see how many aural harmonics we can detect:

There is the second aural harmonic at 300 Hz again. Now let's probe at higher frequencies:

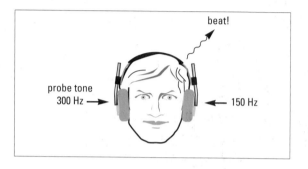

That was the third aural harmonic at three times 150 Hz, or 450 Hz. We're doing all right; let's probe at even higher frequencies:

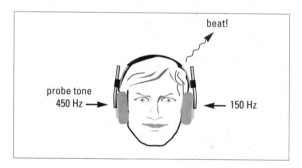

That is the fourth aural harmonic at 600 Hz. This is a very sensitive method of detecting the presence of aural harmonics, but let's move on to considering other types of distortion in the auditory system.

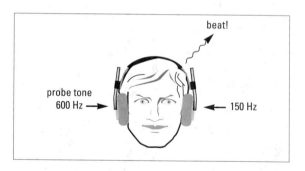

When two tones are introduced into a non-linear system, a series of so-called combination tones is generated. If the higher tone has a frequency H and the lower tone the frequency L, a difference tone of frequency H minus L and a summation tone of the frequency H plus L are produced. These are called the first order sum and difference tones.

The situation becomes much more complex as second order distortion products are considered.

COMBINATION TONES
H = higher frequency
L = lower frequency

Difference tone = H - L
Summation tone = H + L

For example, these include frequencies of 2H minus 2L, 2H minus L, 2L minus H, 2L plus H, and so on. In fact, all these distortion products are similar to what an electronics engineer measures in an amplifier by what is called the *cross-modulation method*.

Combination tone distortion products are as hard to hear as aural harmonics or maybe even harder. For this reason, let's go directly to binaural beats to detect their presence.

For our low frequency L, let us take 700 Hz, and for our high frequency H, we will take 1000 Hz. These two tones will be combined and applied to the left earphone:

To the right earphone we will apply the probe tone, which will be changed through rather wide limits as the experiment progresses. First, we will look for the first order difference tone which should be at a frequency of 1000 Hz minus 700 Hz, or 300 Hz:

As the probe tone goes through 300 Hz, we detect the binaural beat which tells us that, sure enough, the difference tone is present in our heads. This means that some non-linearity in the auditory system is generating this distortion product.

SECOND ORDER
2H - 2L
2H - L
2L - H
2L + H, etc.---

L = 700 Hz
H = 1000 Hz

DIFFERENCE TONE:
H - L = 1000 - 700
= 300 Hz

Summation tones are usually more difficult to detect. The summation tone in this case is 1000 Hz plus 700 Hz, or 1700 hertz. With the probe tone near 1700 Hz, let's see if the first order summation beat is audible:

Well, it's there but much weaker. Let's go on to some of the other combination tone distortion products.

Twice the low frequency minus the high frequency, or 2L minus H, is 1400 Hz minus 1000, or 400 Hz. With this to guide our probe tone, let's see if we can detect this distortion component:

Well, that one is much stronger. Let's try the 2H minus L, which should be at 1300 Hz:

This could go on indefinitely while dozens of combination tone distortion products are located. Instead, let's simply summarize what we have just experienced.

In addition to the simpler aural harmonics which we explored with a single tone injected into our auditory system, we have also detected several combination tones resulting from injecting two tones into the system. With music, many more than two tones fall on the ear simultaneously. Just imagine the horde of aural harmonics and combination tones filling up the audible spectrum!

SUMMATION TONE:
$$H + L = 1000 + 700$$
$$= 1700 \text{ Hz}$$

$$2L - H = (2)(700) - 1000$$
$$= 400 \text{ Hz}$$

$$2H - L = (2)(1000) - 700$$
$$= 1300 \text{ Hz}$$

The masking of higher frequencies by lower ones makes some of these distortion products inaudible. On the other hand, we must remember that distortion products interact with each other, thus creating even more distortion products. But these will be at progressively lower levels.

If you wish, you may now remove your headphones and return to listening with loudspeakers.

What is the source of the non-linearity in our auditory system? The full answer to this question is not yet known, but research is continually revealing bits and pieces of the answer.

One source of non-linearity that is already fairly well known is the middle ear. The three tiny bones of the middle ear, called the ossicles, transmit the vibrations of the eardrum to the oval window of the cochlea. These bones have delicate muscles attached to them which automatically contract when the ear is exposed to very loud sounds. In this way, the transmission of sound through the middle ear is reduced for loud sounds. This is a form of limiter, which most certainly is a non-linear element. It serves to protect the ear from damage from very loud sounds.

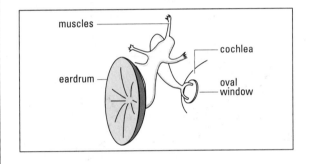

Another possible source of non-linearity is the basilar membrane in the cochlea. As we said before, the cochlea receives the mechanical vibrations from the eardrum by way of the ossicles of the middle ear. It is the cochlea that converts these mechanical vibrations into electrical nerve impulses; these are then sent to the brain by way of the auditory nerve. In this sense, the cochlea is like another well known transducer—the microphone—in that it converts mechanical sound energy into electrical energy.

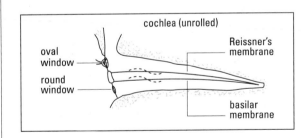

Study of the motions of the basilar membrane of the cochlea indicates that it exhibits what is called *compressive non-linearity*, which operates from the audibility threshold up to maximum sound intensities. That is, it does not act like a limiter or a compressor of the usual type, but rather its compressing action covers its entire range of operation. It is thought that the tremendous dynamic range of the ear is largely due to this very action of the inner ear.

Undoubtedly, further research will reveal other sources of non-linearity in the human auditory system in addition to the ossicles and the basilar membrane we have mentioned.

In summary, we can say that when modest levels of sound fall on our ears, all of these distortion products generated in our heads are at very low levels. For louder sounds, however, the levels of distortion do become appreciable. In other words, at low levels, the ear is quite linear; at high levels, there is a departure from linearity.

The Perception of Delayed Sounds
How we hear echoes and reflections

Talk

Tech

We shall begin this demonstration by repeating an experiment made by Joseph Henry in 1849. He was a scientist and the first secretary of the Smithsonian Institution. The U.S. Congress asked Henry to collaborate in the design of an auditorium for the new Smithsonian building. He was concerned about echoes in the auditorium, so as a scientist, he set out to perform some echo experiments. One of the first was to go outside and listen intently to the echoes of his handclaps from the wall of a building.

Now, we are going to repeat Henry's experiment. As a sound source, Henry clapped his hands, but we'll use a clapboard, the traditional tool for synchronizing picture and sound in the Hollywood film industry. This will provide a more repeatable sound.

We are now in an open field 40 feet from the wall of a large building. Notice the distinct echoes from a 40-foot distance as I clap the boards:

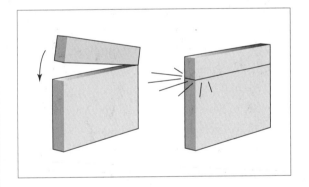

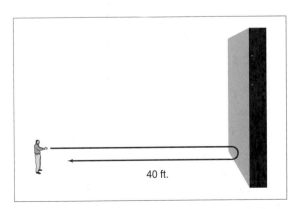

40 ft.

Now we have moved in to a distance of 20 feet from the wall. At this distance, we still hear an echo, but it will be somewhat less distinct:

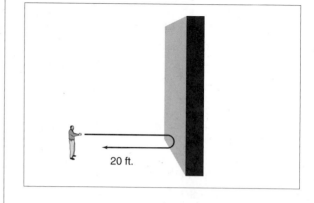

We have now moved in until we are only ten feet from the wall. At the distance of ten feet, the echo has become inaudible:

What happened to the echo?

It must still be there, but we don't really hear it!

The echo is no longer distinct because of the amazing integrating effect of our auditory system. This is called the *Haas Effect* by audio engineers and the *precedence effect* by psychologists.

We shall now leave Joseph Henry and turn to the work of Helmut Haas. We'll duplicate Haas' brilliant, yet very simple experiment, which was a part of his doctoral dissertation at the University of Goettingen in Germany. Conducted in 1949, this was just 100 years after Henry's experiment.

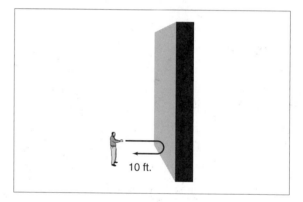

Undoubtedly, your stereo equipment is already adjusted properly, but just to be on the safe side and to avoid spoiling the experiment, let's run a couple of tests that will assure that we get the same results Haas did.

First, we'll check to make sure your two loudspeakers are connected with the same polarity:

That sound is coherent pink noise applied to the right and left channels at equal levels. Listen to this signal again and notice carefully where the noise seems to come from:

If the noise appeared to come from the normal center "image" position between the loudspeakers, your two loudspeakers are connected with the same polarity. If sound seemed to come from all sides, you need to reverse the leads to one of your loudspeakers.

Next, listen to my voice and adjust your balance control to center the "phantom image" exactly between the two loudspeakers.

Now we are all ready to walk through Herr Doctor Haas' fascinating experiment. If you want to duplicate Haas' geometry, the observer was 10 feet from the loudspeakers, which were about 8 feet apart. This makes an angle of about 45 degrees with the observer split by the center line.

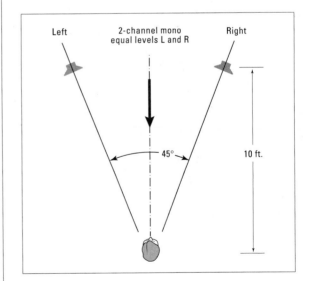

Talk   **Tech**

We shall designate the left loudspeaker as the source of the primary sound and the right loudspeaker as the delayed or echo sound. Identical signals will come from each loudspeaker, but that which comes from the right loudspeaker will be delayed by varying amounts, using a digital delay device.

As I am speaking, the sound from the right loudspeaker is being delayed a very small amount—one-half millisecond. This is only five ten-thousandths of a second or, stated another way, only 500 microseconds. Notice that the image of my voice has shifted from the center to the left loudspeaker, even though the same power is being radiated by both. By delaying the sound of the right speaker very slightly, the sound of the left loudspeaker arrives at your ears ahead of that from the right loudspeaker.

This illustrates the Law of the First Wavefront—that is, the first sound to arrive at your ears determines the subjective impression of direction of arrival of the sound.

Now, just what does this really mean?

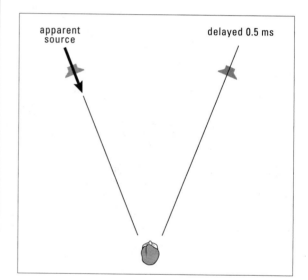

In a modest-sized space like your living room, a classroom, a studio, or a control room, if someone speaks to you from across the room, you have no difficulty sensing the direction of the voice, even if you are blindfolded. That is because the direct sound, which arrives first, gives the directional cue even though followed by an avalanche of reflected sounds. The first sound to arrive tells us from which direction it comes: This is the Law of the First Wavefront. And it all happens in a fraction of a thousandth of a second.

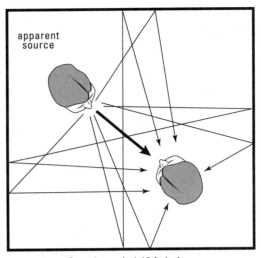

Sound travels 1.13 ft. in 1 ms

Remember that identical power is still being radiated by each loudspeaker. To prove this, while I am talking, place your ear close to each loudspeaker to compare their loudness. Even though equal power is being radiated by each loudspeaker, the sound seems to come entirely from the left, or the primary, loudspeaker when you are back in the central-listening position. The only thing that has been done is to delay the sound from the right loudspeaker a mere one-half millisecond.

The sound of my voice from the right loudspeaker is now being delayed ten thousandths of a second, or ten milliseconds. The sound still appears to come from the left, or primary, loudspeaker.

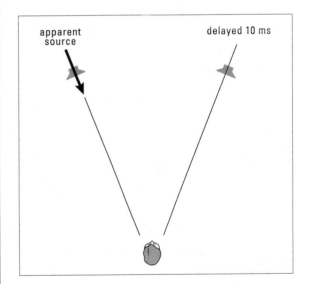

But wait a minute! Something more than just a shift in direction to the left loudspeaker is actually happening.

By switching the delay in and out, we note that the sound is apparently louder with the delay than without it. Listen carefully.

The ten-millisecond delay is now out of the circuit, and as I talk, you hear my voice to be very normal and it appears to come from the normal center image position between the loudspeakers.

The ten-millisecond delay is now back on, and you hear the sound from the left loudspeaker. It also seems to be louder, and there is a certain pleasant change in the character of the sound as well.

We now ask the question, "Is it possible to shift the image back to its central location by increasing the level of the right loudspeaker?" Let's try it.

We have now increased the level of the right loudspeaker 5 dB. The sound still seems to come from the left loudspeaker.

The signal going to the right loudspeaker has now been increased another 5 dB. With the right loudspeaker level increased a total of 10 dB higher than the left, both loudspeakers appear to have more or less the same loudness. Now, the left and right loudspeakers seem to emit sound from their respective directions, but there is still no central image.

Because of room acoustics and human ears differing from person to person, this 10-dB increase might not result in equal sound from left and right loudspeakers for everyone, but it does on the average.

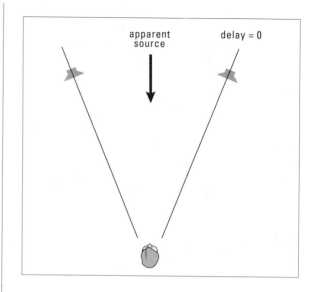

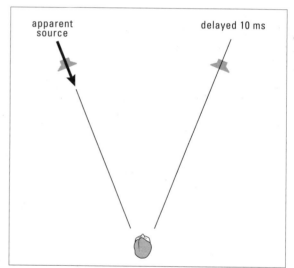

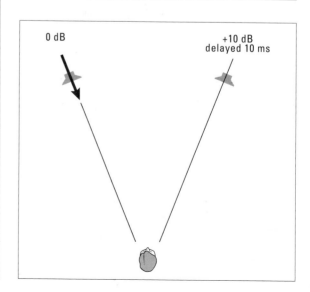

Remember, the sound of the right loudspeaker is still being delayed ten milliseconds. Reducing the level of the right loudspeaker back to equal that of the left once more makes the sound appear to come from the undelayed left channel.

The very distinct echo which you now hear is the result of increasing the delay in the right loudspeaker from 10 milliseconds to 100 milliseconds, or one-tenth of a second.

We have now exceeded the integrating or fusion time of the human ear, and we hear the delayed sound as a discrete echo. The primary sound still seems to come from the left loudspeaker and the echo from the right. The intelligibility of speech is much poorer in the presence of such echoes.

Now, back to normal. What does this show us? For a delay of ten milliseconds, we heard no echo, but at 100 milliseconds we did. In a physical sense, the echo is as real with one as with the other, but because of an important characteristic of our ear/brain system, we hear no echoes with the shorter delays.

Let's review what happens with delays between zero and 100 milliseconds.

With no delay, the very familiar stereo image is in its proper place centered directly between the loudspeakers.

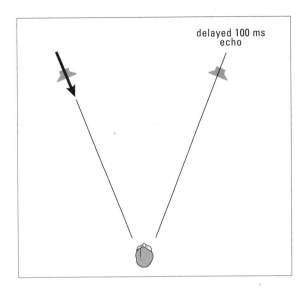

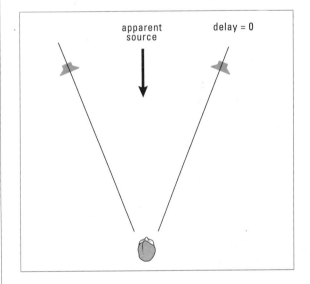

We have again delayed the sound in the right loudspeaker one-half millisecond and immediately the sound jumps to the left loudspeaker, because the sound from it reaches our ears first. This is the Law of the First Wavefront.

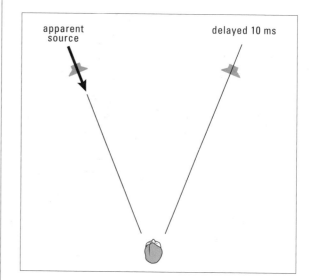

The delay has now been increased to ten milliseconds. Note the increase in apparent loudness and the pleasant change in "liveness" and "body" of the sound. But there is still no apparent echo, even though the ten-millisecond echo delay is present. The ear is fusing the echo with the undelayed sound.

The delay has now been increased to 20 milliseconds, and the sound appears the same as with a 10-millisecond delay. The integrating effect is still completely and thoroughly at work.

The delay is now 30 milliseconds. My voice still seems to come from the left loudspeaker, and no real significant change is noticed except that there is a hint of a discrete echo but not enough to be disturbing.

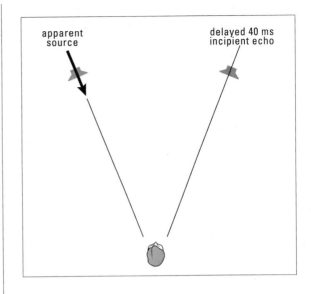

Now the sound to the right loudspeaker is being delayed 40 milliseconds and we note some very definite changes. The apparent loudness has decreased and the delay is beginning to sound like a genuine echo. The integrating effect of the ear/brain system is beginning to break down.

With a delay of 100 milliseconds, the sound from the right loudspeaker is now a discrete echo and we have lost the integrating effect completely. The echo has become a serious disturbance to the sound coming from the left loudspeaker. We will now return to zero time delay.

To review, we have found that very small delays—on the order of even a half millisecond—steer the sound image in the direction of the earlier source, even though both loudspeakers are emitting the same sound at the same level.

With delays greater than 30 milliseconds, a discrete echo begins to be perceived and delays of 50 milliseconds or more result in complete echo dominance.

Everything we have done so far is with speech. Although the basic fusion effects still apply, other types of signals will give different results.

In this next demonstration, we will compare the sound of a chamber group with no delay and with a 30-millisecond delay applied to the right loudspeaker.

First, with no delay:

And now with a 30-millisecond delay:

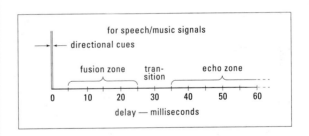

The effect of a 30-millisecond delay on music is very similar to that of speech. We note that the sound image shifts to the left loudspeaker and that there is an apparent increase in loudness. Also, a certain fullness and body is added. Experience has shown that our ears respond to both speech and music in a similar way with regard to delay.

Now, let's try the same zero delay and 30-millisecond delay on snare drum sounds.

First, no delay:

Now with a 30-millisecond delay:

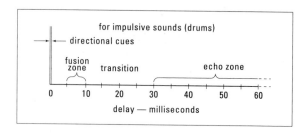

With the drum sound, the 30-millisecond delay creates total confusion. This is because impulsive sounds tolerate much less delay before discrete echoes set in. In fact, while discrete echoes of speech become discernible with a delay of around 40 milliseconds, echoes of single, short-duration impulse sounds will be audible with delays as short as four milliseconds. Sustained, or slowly varying sounds, on the other hand, may require a delay of as much as 80 milliseconds before discrete echoes are noticeable.

A famous musician once said, "There is no such thing as good music outdoors." He had in mind the reflections from the walls and other surfaces of the concert hall which become very much a part of the music. The lack of such reflected energy outdoors, in his opinion, degraded the quality of the music.

It is the integrating effect of the ear which accounts for the difference between sound heard indoors and the same sound heard outdoors.

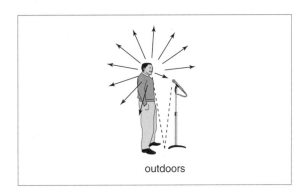

outdoors

I am now outdoors with the microphone about two feet from my mouth. You will notice that my voice sounds a bit flat and dead. The only reflected energy following the direct sound is a small amount reflected from the ground.

I am now in a typical living room with the microphone again about two feet from me. The sound is now well rounded and has a fullness which sounds natural and pleasing to us.

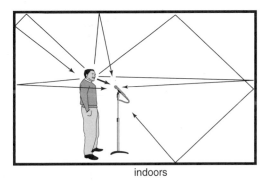

indoors

Indoors, a torrent of reflections follows the direct sound and our ears meticulously gather this later arriving, reflected energy and integrate it with the direct sound. This increases the apparent loudness of the sound and gives it that "indoor" quality. It's a sound we are accustomed to and we have grown to like it.

Normal living rooms are small enough to insure that most of the reflected energy arrives well within the fusion time and is therefore successfully integrated with the direct sound. In large spaces, however, reflections arriving 40 milliseconds or more after the direct sound are perceived as discrete echoes which can be very annoying. But that is another story. In this lesson, we have been primarily interested in sound energy arriving at our ears during the first 20 or 30 milliseconds, which is integrated in a helpful, constructive way.

Why Some Sounds Are More Pleasant Than Others

Consonance, dissonance, and the critical band

Beautiful music is capable of reaching deeply into our souls, imparting peace and tranquillity.

There is something satisfying about musical sounds that blend and harmonize.

Some combinations of sound, however, are anything but pleasant to our ears.

We are going to examine some of the characteristics of our ear/brain hearing system to find out why some intervals sound lovely and some sound raucous and unpleasant.

Music involves such highly complex sounds that one tends to be overwhelmed when trying to analyze just what is going on. For this reason, we must once more fall back on pure tones as we probe into the question of why some tonal combinations sound good and some do not.

Talk   **Tech**

We shall base this exercise on a tone of 500 Hz at a comfortable listening level:

We are now going to add a second tone, an identical 500 Hz of the same amplitude:

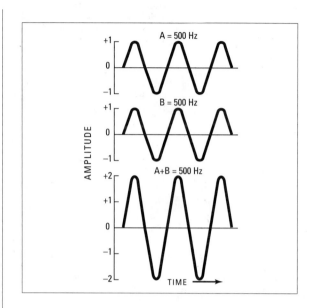

Notice that there is considerable increase in loudness because the two sine waves have a time relationship described as being *in phase*.

Because the two tones are in phase, they add constructively and the resulting combination has twice the amplitude of either tone alone. Those knowledgeable in electronics will recognize this as producing a 6-dB increase in signal level.

Now, let's see what happens if the same two 500-Hz sine waves are combined *out of phase* or in *phase opposition*, that is, when one waveform goes positive, the other goes negative, and vice versa.

First, one signal alone:

And now the second tone will be added momentarily and then taken away:

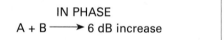

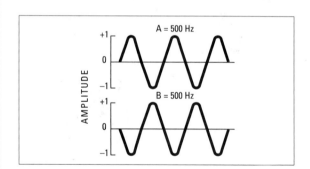

That four-second dead spot in the middle was caused by adding the second equal 500-Hz tone out of phase. When the two signals are in phase opposition, one cancels the other out and the resultant output is zero.

So far, we have been talking about signals with the same frequency. When two tones of differing frequency are combined, some very interesting things happen that have a direct bearing on musical sounds. A tone of 500 Hz added to a tone of 501 Hz sounds like this:

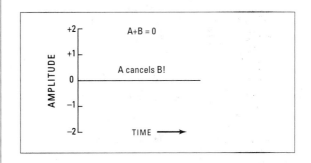

The two tones, only 1 Hz apart, alternately combine in phase and in phase opposition to produce a 1-Hz beat. By holding the 500-Hz tone constant and changing the frequency of the second tone, the beat frequency can be varied at will:

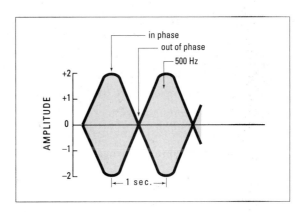

The frequency of the beat is determined by the difference between the frequencies of the two tones which are beating together. Thus, if a tone of either 490 Hz or 510 Hz is combined with the 500-Hz tone, a beat of 10 Hz is produced.

As the difference between the two tones is increased so that the beat frequency increases to about 20 Hz, the ear becomes unable to discern the individual beats:

Talk

Tech

As the beat frequency is increased beyond 20 Hz, a harsh, rattling sound is heard:

Note this roughness well! It is the secret ingredient of what we consider to be unpleasant musical effects, as we shall see later.

As with so many other factors of human hearing, the critical band seems to be involved in how we hear two tones which are sounded together. If the two tones are a critical bandwidth apart, they are heard not as beats or roughness but resolved harmoniously as two separate tones. In the following example, notice the transition from beats, through roughness, to a more pleasant sound, as the two combined tones are increasingly separated in frequency:

To avoid the distraction of the beats and the region of roughness, and for the ear to separate the two tones, they must be at least a critical bandwidth apart.

All this leads us to the conclusion that when several tones are sounded simultaneously, the result may be considered as either pleasant or unpleasant. Another way of describing these sensations is with the terms *consonant* and *dissonant*. In this psychoacoustical context, when we say consonance, we mean tonal or sensory consonance. This is distinguished from the musician's use of the word, which is dependent on frequency ratios and musical theory. Here, we are referring to human perception. Of course, in an ultimate sense, the two definitions must come together. The audibility of these roughness effects does not depend on musical training.

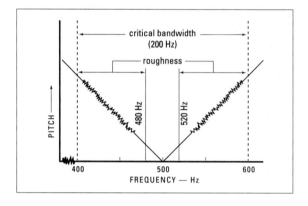

Critical bandwidth calculated from:
ERB = equiv. rectangular band
ERB = 6.23 f^2 + 93.39 f + 28.52 (Hz)
   f = frequency in kHz

Ref.: Moore and Glasberg, J. Acous. Soc. Am., 74, 3, 750 (1983)

Now, instead of frequency, let us consider the same beating effect between two tones in terms of their separation in fractions of a critical bandwidth. As we have seen, at 500 Hz, the critical band is somewhere around 100 Hz wide. Let us define 100 Hz as *unity* and consider fractions of that band.

When two tones have zero separation, they sound as a single tone which has maximum consonance and minimum dissonance:

That is point number one on our curve.

And now, here are the two tones separated by about one-fourth of a critical bandwidth:

This is the least consonant, or the most dissonant, sound.

When the two tones are separated by about one-half a critical bandwidth, the roughness has partially receded to give us about 40 percent of full consonance:

At a separation of about three-fourths of a critical bandwidth, a further improvement in consonance to about 80 percent is noted:

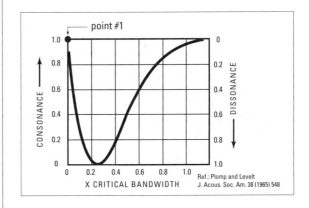

When two notes separated by a full critical bandwidth are combined, 100 percent consonance results:

This puts the effect of combining two tones in proper perspective. If their frequencies are separated by a critical bandwidth or more, the effect is consonant. If less than a critical band separates the tones, varying degrees of dissonance are heard. The most dissonant (that is, the least consonant) spacing of two tones is about one-fourth of a critical bandwidth.

Musicians define an octave as a musical interval whose two tones are separated by eight scale tones:

Tones separated by an octave have an essential similarity recognized by everyone. There is a very good reason for the octave's consonance, which directs our attention once more to the critical band.

An octave represents a frequency ratio of two to one. For example, the frequency of the C an octave above middle C is twice the frequency of middle C:

This means that the harmonics of both are either well separated or coincident up through the audible spectrum when the two are played together:

In fact, the sound of the higher note reinforces that of the lower one. The result is consonance—full, rich, and complete.

THE OCTAVE	
C	C′
Freq. — Hz	Freq. — Hz
261	
523	523
785	
1046	1046
1308	
1570	1570
1831	
2093	2093

Let us try another two-note interval, middle C:

And the G above middle C:

Playing C and G together gives a very pleasant effect:

Musicians call this interval the *perfect fifth* because the two notes are five notes apart:

The perfect fifth is only slightly less pleasant than the octave interval. Let us examine the reasons for such a high degree of consonance.

The fundamentals of C and G are separated by 170 Hz, which is far greater than the critical bandwidth in that frequency range. So far, so good, as this meets the criterion for consonance.

The second harmonics of C and G are 265 Hz apart, a separation some three times the width of the critical band. This also is on the side of consonance.

As the harmonics of C and G are examined closely, we note that they are either separated more than a critical bandwidth or they are at essentially the same frequency, both factors contributing to consonance.

After all, if two harmonics are at the same frequency, they really are a single tone. If they are only a few Hz apart, a beat is superimposed on that frequency which has a positive musical value.

THE PERFECT FIFTH	
C	G
Freq. — Hz	Freq. — Hz
261	
	392
_____	
523	
785	784
1046	
1308	1176
1570	1567
1831	
2093	1959

169

With a renewed sense of getting close to something really significant musically, let's apply these critical band criteria to another musical interval, a minor seventh. The minor seventh can involve middle C again:

And the B-flat above middle C:

Playing these two notes together gives us a minor seventh interval:

While considered by musicians a less consonant interval than the perfect fifth, it is nonetheless a useful tool in the composer's toolbox.

Let's see if we can discover the reason why the minor seventh is considered less consonant than the perfect fifth.

Comparing the frequencies of the fundamentals and harmonics of middle C and B-flat, we fail to find coincident pairs as we did with the perfect fifth interval.

For example, the second harmonic of C and the fundamental of B-flat are 57 Hz apart. The critical bands are about 75 Hz wide in this frequency range. This means that this interval is about three-fourths of a critical bandwidth. It will only have about 80 percent of full consonance.

The fourth harmonic of C and the second harmonic of B-flat are separated 114 Hz, or about nine-tenths the width of a critical band. It is not fully consonant but close.

The fifth harmonic of C and the third harmonic of B-flat are about 90 Hz apart. This means a separation of less than a critical bandwidth—in fact, about 50 percent of a critical band. This interval contributes only half of the full consonance, which means half dissonance as well.

MINOR SEVENTH		
C		B^b
Freq. — Hz		Freq. — Hz
261		
523	57 Hz	466
785 ——		——
1046 ———	114 Hz ———	932
1308	90 Hz	1398
1570 ——		——
1831	34 Hz	1865
2093		

For a fourth example, we can compare the seventh harmonic of C with the fourth harmonic of B-flat. We find them only 34 Hz apart or about 15 percent of a critical bandwidth. This pair is close to being totally dissonant and would certainly contribute some roughness to the combination.

For a minor seventh interval, we find numerous harmonics of C and B-flat close enough together to result in some roughness. Evaluating the separation of harmonics, we find many near misses which are not coincident but less than a critical bandwidth apart contributing to the roughness. Of course, there are many other harmonics which are spaced far more than a critical bandwidth which are fully consonant.

We see that the perfect fifth is close to perfect—that is, close to the consonance of the octave interval. The minor seventh has some intervals separated less than a critical bandwidth, hence, somewhat dissonant.

We conclude that the critical band approach has value in explaining, or even predicting, the degree of consonance an interval exhibits.

Is dissonance necessarily bad? We offer no value judgment on that here. Dissonance can be considered another dimension of musical creativity to be explored. The music of some ethnic groups is more dissonant than ours, and even within our own musical culture, some composers are noted for the degree of dissonance in their works.

Our purpose in this analysis is only to relate consonance and dissonance to the critical bands of the human auditory system.

How We Locate Sounds
The head, the pinna, and an amazing computer

Talk

Tech

The human ear/brain mechanism is extremely effective in localizing the source of a sound. The processes employed are very complex, and even today, only partially understood. This unit will explore this amazing mechanism. First, we will briefly consider some of the better-understood cues the ear uses in sensing the sounds of our environment.

The most dependable cues are those obtained by comparing sounds reaching the two ears. Directional information is contained in a comparison of the relative levels of sound falling on the two ears.

To demonstrate this, we will use bands of random noise one-third octave wide. We use noise instead of tones in order to minimize room effects due to standing waves.

The following sound comes only from the left loudspeaker; the right loudspeaker is silent:

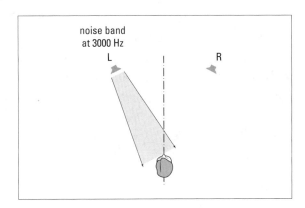

The sound striking your left ear is slightly louder than that falling on your right ear because it is a little closer to the loudspeaker. You may scarcely be able to notice the difference, but there is enough difference in level for your ear to detect it. Thus, you sense the sound coming from the left.

Now, turn your body to the right so that your left ear points directly toward the left loudspeaker. The sound reaching your right ear must travel considerably farther now because your head is a solid barrier to the sound, if you will pardon the expression. Note the louder sound in your left ear:

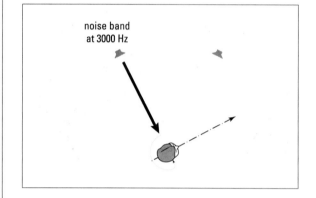

noise band at 3000 Hz

Now a complicating factor enters at this point. How your solid head affects the sound in the far ear depends on the frequency of the sound. With a noise band centered on 8000 Hz, your head is large compared to the wavelength of the sound, and your head will cast a deep shadow of sound at your right ear:

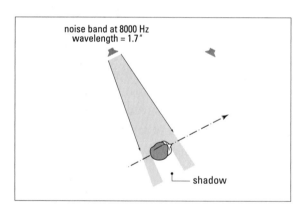

noise band at 8000 Hz
wavelength = 1.7"

shadow

At low frequencies, the sound bends around your head by diffraction and there is very little shadow effect. For example, a band of noise centered on 500 Hz has a wavelength about four times the diameter of your head. Thus, the sound will be almost as loud at your right ear as the closer left ear because of the diffraction of sound around your head:

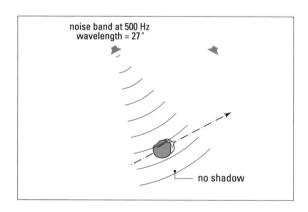

noise band at 500 Hz
wavelength = 27"

no shadow

In this next experiment, wide-band white noise will be used. Remain in the same position and listen carefully to the voice so that spectral changes can be evaluated later:

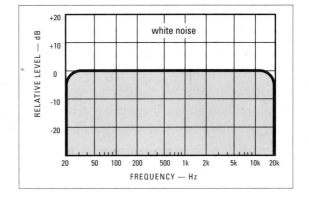

This little experiment will demonstrate that your head casts more of a shadow for high-frequency than for low-frequency sound.

Now, please move closer to the left loudspeaker, say, about two feet from it. This will minimize the effect of room reflections. Once more, aim your left ear at the left loudspeaker as we listen again to wide-band noise:

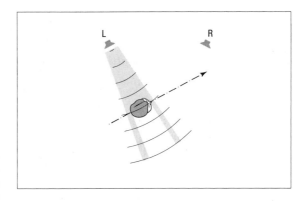

Your left ear receives the noise signal with balanced lows and highs, but the sound at your right ear is quite deficient in highs. Now, maintaining the same position, plug your left ear with your finger as you listen to the same wide-band noise with your right ear alone:

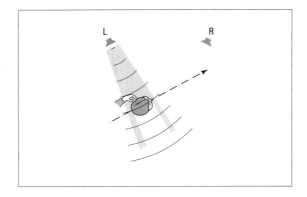

Did you notice a dominance of the bass frequencies and lack of highs in the noise when heard by your right ear alone?

It is relatively easy to hear spectrum changes in wide-band noise, but the same changes can be heard in orchestral music as well. While you are still close to the left loudspeaker, listen to the music both with your finger in your left ear and without it. Experiment a bit as the music continues:

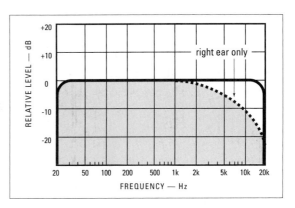

With your finger in your ear, the music still had plenty of bass, but the treble was thin and emaciated because of the shadow cast by your head. This emphasizes the fact that the spectrum of sound falling on each of our two ears may differ greatly. It is these frequency-dependent loudness differences which provide our ears with cues to the location of the source of sound.

Another cue used by the ear to localize sound sources is based on the time of arrival of sound at the two ears. If a sound source is directly in front, directly behind, or directly above our heads, both ears receive identical information in terms of level and time relationships. The result is ambiguity and uncertainty in deciding the direction from which the sound is coming. Moving the head will usually provide changing cues which can resolve this uncertainty.

If a sound arrives at one ear later than the other, we say that there is a phase difference between the two signals. Impulses sent to the brain through the auditory nerve are sorted out and analyzed and these phase shifts are interpreted in terms of direction to the sound source. Many researchers have questioned the sensitivity of our auditory system to phase changes. For these time directional cues to work, however, the ear *must* have the ability to sense phase changes. The big question is: Does the ear really discern phase changes? Let's look into this.

In the previous unit, we discussed beats and their relationship to consonance and dissonance of sounds. Those beats are strictly a physical phenomenon, occurring outside our bodies as the two tones pull in and out of phase. Such external, physical beats may be perceived by one ear.

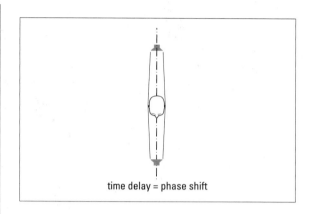

time delay = phase shift

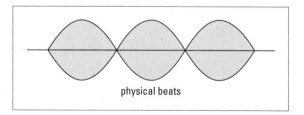

physical beats

There are also so-called *binaural beats* which are strictly subjective or psychophysical. These give evidence that our ears do indeed perceive phase differences.

There will be a brief pause now while you put on your headphones in order to hear some binaural beats. These exist only in your head; they cannot be read by meters, shown on an oscilloscope or even in drawings. You can only hear them in your head.

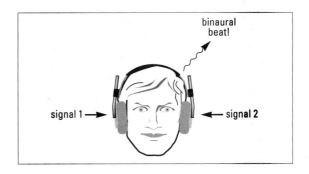

With your headphones now in place and the loudspeakers turned off, a tone of 500 Hz will now be played only in your left earphone:

Another tone, close to 500 Hz, will now be introduced in your right earphone:

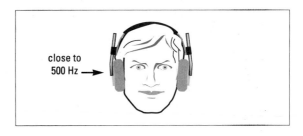

Now, both tones will be sent to their respective ears at the same time:

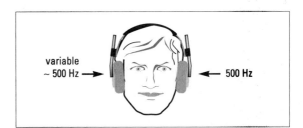

Talk   **Tech**

The subjective beats sound quite different from physical beats and are considered to be evidence that directional phase differences are heard in our heads. They are resolved at the level of neuron discharges in the auditory nerve.

Two ears are required for these comparisons of levels or time of arrival of sounds. It is still possible, however, to locate the source of sounds with a single ear, or as the psychoacoustician would say, monaurally.

Keep your headphones on, and we will determine what sort of cues the single ear uses to provide spatial sensations. We'll use an octave band of noise centered on 8000 Hz. This band of noise extends from about 5600 to 11,300 Hz. It is at these high frequencies that such cues are produced. This octave band of random noise centered on 8000 Hz sounds like this:

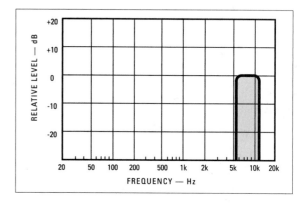

This noise will be sent to your left earphone only. There will be no signal in the right earphone.

We suggest that you shut your eyes and see if you can sense anything about the location of the source of this noise. We'll call this Test A:

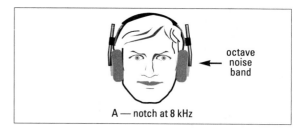

A — notch at 8 kHz

Now, in Test B, a change will be made in the sound. Try to tell where the noise is coming from:

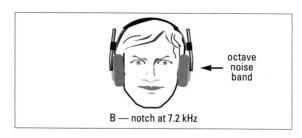

B — notch at 7.2 kHz

In the following Test C, another change will be made. Note the effect on the direction from which the noise seems to come:

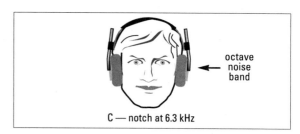

C — notch at 6.3 kHz

Talk   **Tech**

Does it seem that the sound comes from above in Test A?:

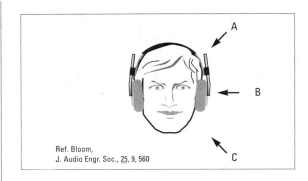

Ref. Bloom,
J. Audio Engr. Soc., 25, 9, 560

Does the sound seem to come directly from the side in Test B?:

Does the sound seem to come from below in Test C?:

These are the sensations that most people experience.

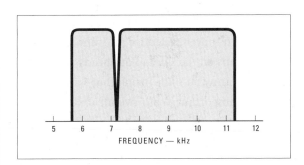

Now, how was the direction that the sound seemed to come from changed? Understanding this helps us to understand what sort of cues a single ear uses and how such cues are generated.

All that was done in Tests A, B, and C was to take a notch out of the noise spectrum. We simply changed the center frequency of this notch. For example, in Test A, the notch was positioned at 8000 Hz:

For Test B, the notch was moved down to 7200 Hz:

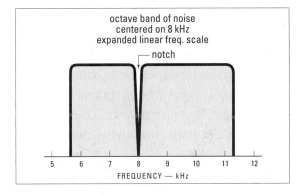

Similarly, in Test C, the notch was moved down still further to 6300 Hz:

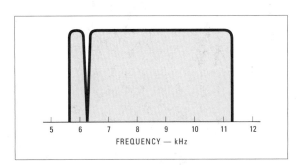

To aid your hearing these differences, we will now sweep the notch from low to high, then stop at each point, and finally sweep it again. Listen for the apparent height of the noise to change:

What is so significant about notching out parts of the signal spectrum we are listening to? Why does it give us cues as to the source location?

This is rather a complex subject, but suffice it to say that it points out the very important role played by the outer ear, the pinna. Those folds of the outer ear reflect sound into the ear canal, and these reflections then combine with the sound entering the ear canal directly, without reflection, creating constructive interference at certain frequencies and destructive interference at other frequencies. In other words, when the two signals are out of phase with each other, there is virtual cancelation, creating a deep notch like we have been simulating. Changing the angle or arrival of sound moves the frequency of the notch.

So, let us never minimize the importance of those flaps on the sides of our heads. They may look funny on some people, but they are extremely important in our overall ability to locate sources of sound.

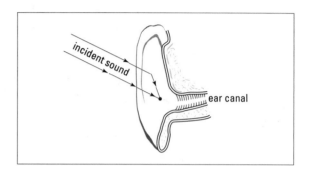

True Binaural Listening

The dummy head in binaural recording

Talk **Tech**

For the first part of this section, you should be listening over your loudspeaker.

The theme for this unit is very simple: *Two ears are better than one*! Everyone knows that, but do we really appreciate fully the tremendous benefits we enjoy every day by having two ears? Let's look into this a bit before we experience true binaural sound with dummy head recording.

It is possible for us to direct our attention toward a desired source of sound as our mind rejects interfering sounds. For example, in a crowd of people, we can converse with one person successfully in spite of a din of competing voices:

This ability is often called the cocktail party effect.

As we listen to polyphonic music, it is possible to *attend* to one melodic strain in the presence of others. When you think about it, it is rather remarkable that we are able to direct our attention to just a part of the mixture of sound falling on our ears, rejecting the rest or at least pushing it into the background.

Talk   **Tech**

Let's try a little experiment to exercise this ability.

Here is an 800-Hz tone which will be one of our signals:

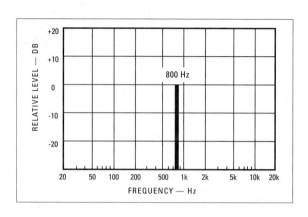

And this is our second signal, a 1200-Hz tone:

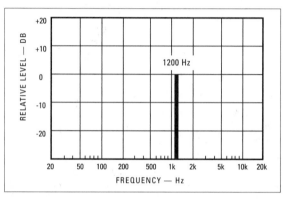

These two tones will be alternated. Let's get used to this signal as it is very rapidly switched from one tone to the other:

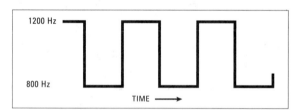

Now, let's try exercising our brain's power of focusing attention. First, concentrate all your attention on the higher tone, excluding the lower:

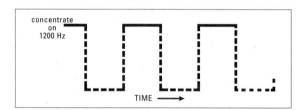

Now, we are going to concentrate our attention on the lower tone, excluding the higher:

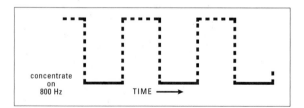

This is listening selectively.

Now, let's listen comprehensively, concentrating on both tones at the same time:

In the following 20 seconds, concentrate your mind first on one, and then on the other, and then on both at the same time:

The selectivity in attentiveness we have just done consciously, we do unconsciously all the time. Perhaps you don't hear the refrigerator, or the neighbors, or the plumbing noises while listening to your hi-fi playing softly. Or we hear the airplane overhead only when our attention is called to it. Or we tune out a noisy colleague because of our immersion in a good book.

For the balance of this section, you should be wearing headphones in order to achieve proper results from the listening tests.

You are now hearing my voice being recorded through the artificial ears of an anthropomorphic mannequin, or as it is commonly called, a dummy head. His name is Fritz, and he comes from Germany. His head and ears are proportioned very carefully and scientifically. Inside his head there is a high-quality microphone at each eardrum position.

Each microphone feeds one channel of a two-channel recording you are now listening to with your headphones. If reproduced through loudspeakers, the sound impressions are almost identical to those obtained by means of conventional stereo microphone techniques, with an increased sense of depth of the soundstage.

I have walked completely around the dummy head while I have been talking to you. Did it seem that I was walking around you? The sound you are hearing is almost identical to that you would hear if you were sitting where the dummy head is located.

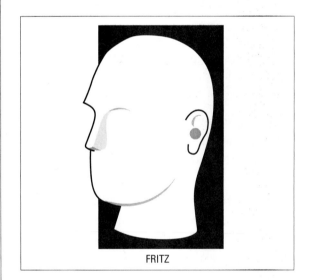

FRITZ

Just to demonstrate the remarkable possibilities of true binaural recording, I shall wander around the studio with my trusty tambourine:

I am now immediately opposite Fritz's left ear:

Now, I am directly behind Fritz:

Now, I am opposite Fritz's right ear:

Now, I have returned to my position directly in front of Fritz.

Now that we are acquainted with Fritz and his indoor functioning, let's take him outside to sample the world of sounds binaurally:

Here, Fritz is cruising up the tourist section of Demonbruen Street in Nashville, Tennessee:

Now, Fritz is in the back seat of an auto with conversation going on between two persons in the front seat. His window is open for the better sounds of cars and trucks passing by:

Since Fritz has to make a number of personal appearances, we thought it would be nice to have him drop in on a recording session at Studio C Productions in Nashville:

We are now inside the lobby of the historic RCA Studio B, which is now being administered by the Country Music Hall of Fame, as a group of tourists is wandering in to explore the birthplace of the Nashville sound:

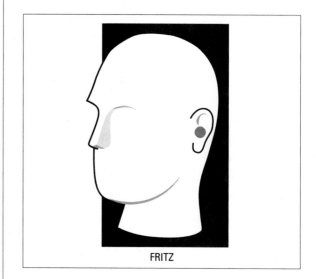

FRITZ

Our ears, if they are in good working condition, give us true binaural listening. There is no recording and reproduction system available today which can truly duplicate the amazing performance of the human auditory system. However, using dummy heads such as Fritz, it is possible to record and reproduce sounds—via headphones of reasonable quality—with excellent naturalness and fidelity and with accurate spatial sense as well.

But there remains much to be done, both in research toward better understanding of human hearing and in the recording and reproducing arts as well.

Glossary

Amplitude The instantaneous amplitude of an oscillating quantity, such as sound pressure, is its value at any instant. The peak value is the maximum value attained. If not specified, the amplitude is usually effective, or root-mean-square value.

Anthropomorphic mannequin A mannequin made in human shape. In this case, a head made for binaural recording with pinnas accurately shaped and a microphone diaphragm placed at each eardrum position.

Attenuate To lessen or decrease in magnitude. In electronic circuitry, a resistance network to control signal amplitudes.

Audiogram A graph showing absolute threshold for pure tones as a function of frequency. It is usually plotted as hearing loss in dB as a function of frequency.

Aural harmonic A harmonic generated by a non-linearity within the auditory apparatus.

Bandwidth A range of frequencies. A filter bandwidth is usually defined as the difference between the low and high frequencies defined by the -3 dB points on the filter response.

Basilar membrane A membrane in the cochlea that vibrates as the ear is excited by sound.

Beats Periodic fluctuations of sound caused by the interaction of two signals close together in frequency. The frequency of the beat is the difference between the frequencies of the two signals.

Binaural Involving two ears in listening.

Binaural beat A beat perceived in the head between two tones, one applied to one ear and the other to the other ear.

Binaural recording A two-channel recording of a binaural signal from a dummy head microphone arrangement.

Chromatic scale The musical scale made up of 13 half tones to the octave.

Circularity of pitch In addition to the rectilinear scale of pitch from one octave to the next, there is the suggestion that the same path may be traced with a circular component via a helical path.

Clipping The reduction or cutting off of signal peaks by a non-linear circuit element.

Cochlea The inner ear that transduces the mechanical energy of sound waves to neural impulses that are sent to the brain.

Combination tone A tone perceived as part of a complex stimulus that is not present in the sensations produced by the constituent parts of the complex stimulus alone. When two tones are introduced into a non-linear system, combination tones are produced that are sum and difference tones and various multiple combinations of the original two tones.

Complex tone A tone composed of fundamental and harmonics, partials or overtones.

Consonance A pleasing combination of musical sounds.

Critical band Auditory bandpass filters revealed by masking and other experiments.

Cross modulation The modulation taking place in a non-linear circuit when two tones are applied. The products resulting are a measure of the non-linearity.

Decibel One-tenth of a bel. A bel is the logarithm of a power ratio. The decibel (abbreviated as dB), being a logarithmic parameter, is useful in auditory work because the ear responds in a somewhat logarithmic fashion. The use of ratios of power or pressure become very unwieldy in hearing experiments.

Diffraction A diffracted sound wave is one whose wavefront has been changed in direction by an obstacle or other non-homogeneity in the medium.

Dissonance An inharmonious sound or combination of sounds.

Distortion A change in waveform.

Dummy head A mannequin made to conform to the shape and size of the human head having microphone diaphragms placed at the position of the eardrums. Used for binaural recording.

Dynamic range The amplitude of the signal handled by a system is limited on the low end by the noise of the system and on the high end by the overload or clipping level The range between is termed the dynamic range of the system.

Equalization The adjustment of the frequency response of a system to achieve a desired response.

Envelope The envelope of any function is a smooth curve going through the peaks of the function.

Equal loudness contour A curve plotted as a function of frequency defining the sound pressure level required to give equal loudness.

Filter A device that modifies the frequency response of a signal, usually in electrical form. Classes of filters include: bandpass filters, band rejection filters, lowpass filters, highpass filters, notch filters, equalization filters, etc.

Free field A sound field free from the effects of boundaries or other irregularities.

Frequency For a periodic wave, frequency is the number of periods or cycles occurring per second. The unit is cycles per second or hertz (abbreviated Hz).

Fundamental frequency The fundamental frequency of a periodic wave is the sinusoidal component having the same period as the periodic wave. The term is applied primarily to the lowest component of a complex wave.

Harmonic The components of a complex wave that are integral multiples of the fundamental. The fundamental is generally called the first harmonic.

Haas effect Delayed replicas of a signal combined with the original signal are heard as echoes if the delay is greater than about 40 milliseconds. For delays up to about 30 milliseconds, the ear integrates the delayed and the original signal with no echo being perceived. This is called the Haas effect, also called the precedence effect.

Hertz See Frequency.

Intensity The sound power transmitted through a given area in a sound field. This is the definition used in acoustics. A popular use of the term is to denote any quantity relating to the amount of sound, such as amplitude, level, pressure, power, etc.

Interference In regard to sound, interference is the pattern resulting from the vector combination of one or more sound waves. Destructive interference is the result of out-of-phase combination, whereas constructive interference is the result of in-phase combination.

Law of the first wavefront In a situation in which the ear is bombarded by reflected sound coming from all directions, such as in a room, the first wave arriving at the ear—the direct, unreflected wave—gives the directional cue.

Level The level of a sound is specified in relation to some reference level. See sound pressure level.

Linear A linear system is one in which a signal may pass through with no distortion.

Loudness This is the level attribute of an auditory sensation in which sounds may be ordered on a scale from quiet to loud.

Loudness level The loudness level in phons is the sound pressure level in dB of a pure tone at a frequency of 1000 Hz. This is a physical, not a subjective measurement.

Masked audiogram A graph of the amount of masking, in dB, produced by a given sound as a function of frequency of the masked sound.

Masking The amount (or the process) by which the threshold of audibility of one sound is raised by the presence of another (masking) sound.

Masking tone The tone, adjustable in frequency, used in a masking experiment, as opposed to the tone or other signal being masked. The probe tone.

Modulation The variation of the amplitude or frequency of a stimulus or signal.

Monaural Involving only a single ear in listening.

Noise In one sense, noise is unwanted sound. White noise has uniform energy throughout the frequency range considered, for example, the audible band. Noise has a normal distribution (Gaussian) of instantaneous amplitudes. See also pink noise.

Noise band A noise of limited spectral content, usually obtained by passing white or other wide-band noise through a bandpass filter.

Non-linear system A system in which the output is not identical to the input. The two differ by the distortion products generated in the system.

Octave The interval between two tones having frequency ratios of 2:1. The upper edge of an octave band centered on a given frequency may be found by multiplying the center frequency by 2 to the ½ power. The lower edge may be found by dividing the center frequency by 2 to the ½ power.

One-third octave (band or filter) One-third octave at a given center frequency is defined as stretching from a lower edge of center frequency divided by 2 to the $\frac{1}{6}$th power to upper edge found by multiplying the center frequency by 2 to the $\frac{1}{6}$th power.

Oscillator A generator of sine wave signals.

Ossicles The bones of the middle ear: the malleus, the inca, and the stapes.

Otologist A medical doctor specializing in the diseases and anatomy of the ear.

Out of phase When the time relationship of two periodic waves are in phase opposition, or out of phase, as the amplitude of one goes in a positive direction, the other goes in a negative direction.

Oval window The footplate of the stapes of the middle ear is the oval window to the cochlea by which sound energy is transmitted to the fluid of the cochlea.

Partial Any sinusoidal frequency component in a complex tone.

Period The smallest time interval over which a function repeats itself.

Periodic sound A sound whose waveform repeats itself regularly as a function of time.

Phase The phase of a periodic waveform is the fractional part of a period through which the waveform has advanced, measured from some arbitrary point in time.

Phon The unit of loudness level.

Pink noise Noise whose spectral amplitude falls off with frequency at a 3 dB per octave rate.

Pinna The outermost, sound-gathering part of the external ear.

Pitch That attribute of auditory sensation by which sounds may be ordered on a musical scale.

Polarity The + and - signs indicative of the direction of flow of an electric current.

Precedence effect See Haas effect.

Psychoacoustics The study of human perception of sound. Studies relating psychology and acoustics.

Pure tone A sound wave whose instantaneous pressure variations as a function of time is a sinusoidal function.

Random noise See White noise.

Rise time The time it takes a transient sound or signal to rise to full value.

Round window The tiny diaphragmatic window in the cochlea opening into the middle ear. It serves as a pressure release of the cochlear fluid as the oval window is actuated.

Sine wave/sinusoidal vibration A waveform whose pressure variation as a function of time is a sine function. It is related to simple harmonic motion such as that of a loudspeaker diaphragm.

Sound pressure level The level of a sound in dB relative to an internationally defined reference level. The accepted reference level for intensity is 10^{-16} watts per sq. cm, for sound pressure is 2×10^{-5} Newtons per sq. meter, which is the same as 20 micropascals.

Spectrum The spectrum of a sound wave is the distribution in frequency of the magnitudes of the components of the wave. It is represented by plotting power, amplitude, or level as a function of frequency.

Spectrum analyzer An electronic device for analyzing the distribution of energy in a signal as a function of frequency. Many such devices display the spectrum of the signal applied to its input in an amplitude-frequency plot.

Square wave A highly truncated sine wave is a square wave. It is a periodic wave whose amplitude is a constant positive or negative value with very fast transition time.

Standing wave When a steady state sine wave signal irradiates an enclosed space, such as an organ pipe or small room, multiple reflections from opposing surfaces set up a stable distribution of sound pressure that is called a standing wave.

Summation tone Combination tone components formed by adding two or more of the combination tone products.

Synthesizer A modern electronic instrument of extreme flexibility in which timbre, attack, decay, and other factors are under the control of the musician.

Timbre That attribute of auditory sensation by which a listener can judge that two sounds of the same loudness and pitch are different. It is a subjective measure of the quality of a sound.

Tone A sound wave capable of stimulating an auditory sensation of pitch.

Tuning curve For a single nerve fiber, a tuning curve is a graph of the lowest sound level at which the fiber will respond, plotted as a function of frequency. A curve of thresholds plotted as a function of frequency.

Vibrato A musical embellishment consisting of a rapid rise and fall of frequency of a tone at about six or seven per second.

Wave analyzer See Spectrum analyzer.

Waveform A description of the shape or form of a wave. Usually a plot against time of the instantaneous amplitudes or pressures.

Wavelength The wavelength of a periodic wave in an isotropic medium is the perpendicular distance between two wavefronts in which the displacements have a difference of phase of one complete cycle.

White noise See Noise.

Bibliography

General

Deutsch, Diana (ed.), *The Psychology of Music*, Academic Press, New York (1982), 542 pp. A compilation of 18 papers (two by the editor). Good summary of the field.

Moore, Brian C.J., *An Introduction to the Psychology of Hearing*, Academic Press, New York (1982). Primarily a student text, well written, fully illustrated.

Pickles, James O., *An Introduction to the Psychology of Hearing*, Academic Press, New York (1982), 341 pp. Primarily a student text, well written, fully illustrated.

Schroeder, Manfred R., *Models of Hearing*, Proc. IEEE, Vol. 63, No. 9 (Sept. 1978) pp. 1332-1352.

Stevens, S.S. and H. Davis, *Hearing, Its Psychology and Physiology*. First published in 1938, republished for the Acoustical Society of America by the Am. Inst. of Physics, New York in 1983. Excellent coverage of the work in auditory perception prior to 1938.

Tobias, Jerry V. (ed.), *Foundations of Modern Auditory Theory*, Vol. 1 (1970) and Vol. 2 (1972), Academic Press, New York. Excellent surveys of the field by leading researchers, but it does not include significant recent advances.

Loudness, Pitch, and Timbre

Fletcher, H., *Loudness, Pitch, and Timbre of Musical Tones and Their Relation to the Intensity, the Frequency, and Overtone Structure*, J. Acous. Soc. Am., Vol. 6 (1934) pp. 59-69.

Masking

Bilger, R.C. and I.J. Hirsh, *Masking of Tones by Bands of Noise*, J. Acous. Soc. Am., Vol. 28, No. 4 (July 1956) pp. 623-630.

Fletcher, H., *Loudness, Masking, and Their Relation to the Hearing Process and the Problem of Noise Measurement*, J. Acous. Soc. Am., Vol. 9 (April 1938) pp. 275-293. Historically important in development of the critical band concept.

Small, Arnold M., *Pure Tone Masking*, J. Acous. Soc. Am., Vol. 31, No. 12 (Dec. 1959) pp. 1619-1625.

The Critical Band

De Boer, E., *Note on the Critical Bandwidth*, J. Acous. Soc. Am., Vol. 34, No. 7 (July 1962) pp. 985-986.

Egan, James P. and Harold W. Hake, *On the Masking Pattern of a Simple Auditory Stimulus*, J. Acous. Soc. Am., Vol. 22, No. 5 (Sept. 1950) pp. 622-630.

Fletcher, H., *Auditory Patterns*, rev. Mod Physics, Vol. 12 (1940) pp. 47-65.

Glasberg, Brian R. and Brian C.J. Moore, *Auditory Filter Shapes in Subjects with Unilateral and Bilateral Hearing Impairments*, J. Acous. Soc. Am., Vol. 79, No. 4 (April 1966) pp. 1020-1033.

Greenwood, Donald D., *Auditory Masking and the Critical Band*, J. Acous. Soc. Am., Vol. 33, No. 4 (April 1961) pp. 484-502.

Haggard, M.P. *Feasibility of Rapid Critical Bandwidth Estimates*, J. Acous. Soc. Am., Vol. 55 (1974) pp. 304-308.

Hawkins, J.E., Jr. and S.S. Stevens, *The Masking of Pure Tones and of Speech by White Noise*, J. Acous. Soc. Am., Vol. 22, No. 1 (Jan. 1950) pp. 6-13.

Houtgast, T., *Auditory Filter Characteristics Derived from Direct Masking Data and Pulsation Threshold Data with a Rippled Noise Masker*, J. Acous. Soc. Am., Vol. 62, No. 2 (Aug. 1977) pp. 409-415.

Johnstone, B.M., K.J. Taylor, and A.J. Boyle, *Mechanics of the Guinea Pig Cochlea*, J. Acous. Soc. Am., Vol. 47, No. 2-Part 2 (1970) pp. 504-509.

Khanna, S.M. and D.G.B. Leonard, *Basilar Membrane Tuning in the Cat Cochlea*, Science, Vol. 215 (15 Jan. 1982) pp. 305-306. Claims that when exceptional precautions are taken to minimize cochlear damage, the basilar membrane tuning curve is closer to neural tuning curves.

Moore, Brian C.J. and Brian R. Glasberg, *Suggested Formulae for Calculating Auditory Filter Bandwidths and Excitation Patterns*, J. Acous. Soc. Am., Vol. 74, No. 3 (Sept. 1983) pp. 750-753.

Patterson, Roy D., *Auditory Filter Shapes Derived with Noise Stimuli*, J. Acous. Soc. Am., Vol. 59, No. 3 (Mar. 1976) pp. 640-654.

Patterson, Roy D. and Ian Nimmo-Smith, *Off-Frequency Listening and Auditory Filter Asymmetry*, J. Acous. Soc. Am., Vol. 67, No. 1 (Jan. 1980) pp. 229-244.

Patterson, Roy D., Ian Nimmo-Smith, Daniel L. Weber, and Robert Mitroy, *The Deterioration of Hearing with Age; Frequency Selectivity, the Critical Ratio, the Audiogram, and Speech Threshold*, J. Acous. Soc. Am., Vol. 72, No. 6 (Dec. 1982) pp. 1788-1803.

Plomp, R., *The Ears As a Frequency Analyzer*, J. Acous. Soc. Am., Vol. 36, No. 9 (Sept. 1964) pp. 1628-1636.

Schafer, T.H., R.S. Gales, C.A. Shewmaker, and P.O. Thompson, *The Frequency Selectivity of the Ear as Determined by Masking Experiments*, J. Acous. Soc. Am., Vol. 22, No. 4 (July 1950) pp. 490-496.

Swets, John A., David M. Green, and Wilson P. Tanner, Jr., *On the Width of Critical Bands*, J. Acous. Soc. Am., Vol. 34, No. 1 (Jan. 1962) pp. 108-113.

Zwicker, E., G. Flottorp, and S.S. Stevens, *Critical Band Width in Loudness Summation*, J. Acous. Soc. Am., Vol. 29, No. 5 (May 1957) pp. 548-557.

Delay, Echoes

Gardner, Mark B., *Historical Background of the Haas and/or Precedence Effect*, J. Acous. Soc. Am., Vol. 43, No. 6 (1968) pp. 1243-1248.

Haas, Helmut, *The Influence of a Single Echo on the Ability of Speech*, J. Audio Engr. Soc., Vol. 20, No. 2 (Mar. 1972) pp. 146-159.

Lochner, J.P.A. and J.F. Burger, *The Subjective Masking of Short Time Delayed Echoes by Their Primary Sounds and Their Contribution to the Intelligibility of Speech*, Acustica, Vol. 8, No. 1 (1958) pp. 1-10.

Muncey, R.W., A.F.B. Nickson, and P. Dubout, *The Acceptability of Speech and Music with a Single Artificial Echo*, Acustica, Vol. 3 (1953) pp. 168-173.

Nickson, A.F.B., R.W. Muncey, and P. Dubout, *The Acceptability of Artificial Echoes with Reverberant Speech and Music*, Acustica, Vol. 4 (1954) pp. 515-518.

Wallach, Hans, Edwin B. Newman, and Mark R. Rosenzweig, *The Precedence Effect in Sound Localization*, J. Audio Engr. Soc., Vol. 21, No. 10 (Dec. 1973) pp. 817-826.

Consonance/Dissonance

Geary, J.M., *Consonance and Dissonance of Pairs of Inharmonic Sounds*, J. Acous. Soc. Am., Vol. 67, No. 5 (May 1980) pp. 1785-1789.

Kameoka, Akio and Mamoru Kuriyagawa, *Consonance Theory Part I: Consonance of Dyads*, J. Acous. Soc. Am., Vol. 45, No. 6 (1969) pp. 1451-1459. *Consonance Theory Part II: Consonance of Complex Tones and Its Calculation Method*, Vol. 45, No. 6 (1969) pp. 1460-1469.

Plomp, R. and W.J.M. Levelt, *Tonal Consonance and Critical Bandwidth*, J. Acous. Soc. Am., Vol. 38 (1965) pp. 548-560.

Localization

Blauert, Jens, *Localization and the Law of the First Wavefront in the Median Plane*, J. Acous. Soc. Am., Vol. 50, No. 2-Part 2 (1971) pp. 466-470.

Blauert, Jens, *Spatial Hearing*, Translated from the German by John S. Allen, MIT Press, Cambridge (1983) 427 pp.

Bloom, P. Jeffrey, *Determination of Monaural Sensitivity Changes Due to the Pinna by Use of Minimum-Audible-Field Measurements in the Lateral Vertical Plane*, J. Acous. Soc. Am., Vol. 61, No. 3 (Mar. 1977) pp. 820-827.

Bloom, P. Jeffrey, *Creating Source Elevation Illusions by Spectral Manipulation*, J. Audio Engr. Soc. Vol. 25, No. 9 (Sept. 1977) pp. 560-565.

Fisher, H. Geoffrey and Sanford J. Freedman, *The Role of the Pinna in Auditory Localization*, J. Auditory Research, Vol. 8 (1968) pp. 15-26.

Gardner, Mark B. and Robert S. Gardner, *Problem of Localization in the Median Plane: Effect of Pinnae Cavity Occulusion*, J. Acous. Soc. Am., Vol. 53, No. 2 (1973) pp. 400-408.

Hartmann, W.M., *Localization of Sound in Rooms*, J. Acous. Soc. Am., Vol. 74, No. 5 (Nov. 1983) pp. 1380-1391.

Mehrgardt, S. and V. Mellert, *Transformation Characteristics of the External Human Ear*, J. Acous. Soc. Am., Vol. 61, No. 6 (June 1977) pp. 1567-1576.

Roffler, Suzanne K. and Robert A. Butler, *Factors That Influence the Localization of Sound in the Vertical Plane*, J. Acous. Soc. Am., Vol. 43, No. 6 (1968) pp. 1255-1259.

Roffler, Suzanne K. and Robert A. Butler, *Localization of Tonal Stimuli in the Vertical Plane*, J. Acous. Soc. Am., Vol. 43, No. 6 (1968) pp. 1260-1266.

Rodgers, C.A.P. *Pinna Transformations and Sound Reproduction*, J. Audio Engr. Soc., Vol. 29, No. 4 (April 1981) pp. 226-234.

Shaw, E.A.G. and R. Teranishi, *Sound Pressure Generated in an External-Ear Replica and Real Human Ears by a Nearby Point Source*, J. Acous. Soc. Am., Vol. 44, No. 1 (1968) pp. 240-249.

Shaw, E.A.G., *Transformation of Sound Pressure Level from the Free Field to the Eardrum in the Horizontal Plane*, J. Acous. Soc. Am., Vol. 56, No. 6 (Dec. 1974) pp. 1848-1861.

Shaw, E.A.G. and M.M. Vaillancourt, *Transformation of Sound Pressure Level from the Free Field to the Eardrum Presented in Numerical Form*, J. Acous. Soc. Am., Vol. 78, No. 3 (Sept. 1985) pp. 1120-1123.

Wright, Donald, John H. Hebrank, and Blake Wilson, *Pinna Reflections as Cues for Localization*, J. Acous. Soc. Am., Vol. 56, No. 3 (Sept. 1974) pp. 957-962.

Miscellaneous

Deer, J.A., P.J. Bloom, and D. Preis, *New Results for Perception of Phase Distortion*, presented at the 77th convention of the Audio Engineering Society (Mar. 1985), preprint #2197.

Hansen, Villy and Erik Rorback Madsen, *On Aural Phase Detection*, Part I, J. Audio Engr. Soc., Vol. 22, No. 1 (Jan./Feb. 1974) pp. 10-14; Part II, Vol. 22, No. 10 (Dec. 1974) pp. 783-788.

Lamore, P.J.J., *Perception of Two-Tone Octave Complexes*, Acustica, Vol. 34, No. 1 (1975) pp. 1-14.

Mathes, R.C. and R.L. Miller, *Phase Effects in Monaural Perception*, J. Acous. Soc. Am., Vol. 19, No. 5 (Sept. 1947) pp. 780-797.

Plomp, R. and H.J.M. Steneeken, *Effects of Phase on the Timbre of Complex Tones*, J. Acous. Soc. Am., Vol. 46 (1969).

Raiford, C.A. and E.D. Schubert, *Recognition of Phase Changes in Octave Complexes*, J. Acous. Soc. Am., Vol. 50 (1971) pp. 557-567.

Schorer, E., *Critical Modulation of Frequency Based on Detection of AM versus FM Tones*, J. Acous. Soc. Am., Vol. 79, No. 4, (Apr. 1966) pp. 1054-1057.

Tonndorf, J., *Localization of Aural Harmonics Along the Basilar Membrane of Guinea Pigs*, J. Acous. Soc. Am., Vol. 30 (1958) pp. 938-943.

Wiener, F.M. and D.A. Ross, *Pressure Distribution in the Auditory Canal*, J. Acous. Soc. Am., Vol. 18 (1946) pp. 401-408.

Index

CD Track List